Kerry V. Kern

The New Terrier Handbook

Everything about Purchase, Care,
Nutrition, Breeding, Behavior, and Training

With Color Photographs by Well-Known Photographers
and Drawings by Michele Earle-Bridges

Consulting Editor: Matthew M. Vriends, PhD

BARRON'S

Photo Credits: American Kennel Club: pages 9, bottom; 110 (bottom)

Jane B. Donahue: page 128 (bottom)

Raymond D. Kopen: page 127 (top, bottom)

Aaron Norman: front cover

Wim Van Vught: inside front cover; pages 9 top; 10 (top, bottom); 19 (top, bottom); 20 (top, bottom); 37 (top, bottom); 38 (top, bottom); 55 (top, bottom); 56 (top, bottom); 73 (top, bottom); 74 (top, bottom); 91 (top, bottom); 92 (top, bottom); 109 (top, bottom); 110 (top); 128; inside back cover; back cover

Advice and Warning: This book is concerned with buying, keeping, and raising terriers. The publisher and the author think it is important to point out that the advice and information for terrier maintenance applies to healthy, normally developed animals. Anyone who buys an adult terrier or one from an animal shelter must consider that the animal may have behavioral problems and may, for example, bite without any visible provocation. Such anxiety-biters are dangerous for the owner as well as for the general public.

Caution is further advised in the association of children with a terrier, in meetings with other dogs, and in exercising the dog without a leash.

About the Author: Kerry Kern, formerly Managing Editor of *Canine Graphic,* has written extensively on the subject of dogs. She is the author of *Labrador Retrievers* (Barron's).

All inquiries should be addressed to:
Barron's Educational Series, Inc.
250 Wireless Boulevard
Hauppauge, NY 11788

International Standard Book No. 0-8120-3951-3

Library of Congress Catalog Card No. 88-3331

Library of Congress Cataloging-in-Publication Data

Kern, Kerry V.
    The new terrier handbook.

    Includes index.
    1. Terriers.   I. Title.
SF429.T3K47 1988   636.7′55   88-3331
ISBN 0-8120-3951-3

Printed in Hong Kong

56   977   987

Contents

Contents

Foreword

Today's terriers are descended from the "earth dogges" of earlier centuries that earned their keep by ridding their masters' homes and fields of vermin and small predators. From this inauspicious beginning emerged a group of dogs with an incredible amount of courage and an unmatched zest for life. Spunk, loyalty, and perseverance are character traits that typify the terrier breeds and set them apart from the rest of the canine world. With the passage of time terriers have adapted to new life styles and few are called upon to perform the services the breeds were once so adept at. The spirit and instincts remain, however.

The dogs grouped together in this book under the heading of "terrier" encompass some thirty distinct breeds, varying in size from one of the smallest, the Yorkshire terrier, to the mighty giant schnauzer. Each breed is unique, but all share some common links.

My terrier breeds are not limited to those currently assigned to the Terrier Group by the official kennel clubs in the United States and England. When I began writing this book, the publisher requested that I include all breeds that share the "terrier" name. While I had previously dismissed such breeds as the Yorkshire and the Boston terriers as not belonging in this text, I soon agreed with the logic of including all dogs that stem from the early terrier lines and share a common heritage.

Although some of the breeds in this book are more accurately "distant cousins" of the Terrier Group members, all earn their place by their instincts and personalities. Physical differences—primarily size—have led some breeds to be classified among other groups. The Yorkshire and silky are designated as Toys; the standard and giant schnauzers are Working dogs; the Boston is a Nonsporting breed. They come from a variety of backgrounds and have a variety of homelands, but the "earth dog" nature remains. The basic terrier temperament and heritage are the unifying factors in this text.

One breed carrying the terrier name, the Tibetan terrier, is not included. It does not descend from recognized terrier strains, does not have the typical terrier disposition, and does not "go to the earth" as terriers do. This ancient breed received the name "terrier" when it was introduced to the Western world primarily because its size was compatible with that of many terriers. A true terrier it is not.

Since I have limited myself to those breeds recognized by the kennel clubs for official breed registration, Jack Russell terriers do not have a section of their own (but a photograph is included, as this breed may some day join the recognized list). A cross of fox and the original English terriers, the Jack Russell has many fans throughout the world. The main drawback toward recognition seems to be a lack of consistent breed type and monitored breedings. Officially recognized or not, these dogs have the spunk and spirit of the true terrier.

I would like to acknowledge the assistance of Matthew Vriends, PhD, consulting editor of this series, and Helgard Niewisch, DVM, who read the manuscript and made invaluable suggestions.

K.V.K.

An Introduction to Terriers

While impossible to document, it is believed that domesticated dogs *(Canis familiaris)* may date back more than 20,000 years. The earliest specimens are thought to have stemmed from ancestors of the wolf family. Both early humans and the forerunners of today's domesticated dog lived a simple existence dominated by the need to hunt to survive. In a mutually satisfactory bond, man supplied all the dog's basic needs and in return the dog aided man in the hunt, in controlling his flocks, and in protecting his home. Over time, man learned how to refine the dog through selective breeding to enhance desired traits. Thus, from these first strains of domestic dog more than 400 distinct breeds have emerged.

Several of the hound breeds have been traced back more than 8,000 years to the time of the pharaohs. Terriers are not nearly as ancient a group, but most can trace their heritage to the British Isles in the 14th century. Similar breeds were also being developed in Germany around this same time. The word "terrier" is derived from *terra*, the Latin word for "earth." Terriers (literally "earth dogs") were originally used to "go to the ground" and hunt out and destroy small vermin. A terrier trails an animal wherever it may go, often digging down into holes and submerged nests. Controlling vermin required an energetic and courageous animal with a well-developed sense of smell—a dog could hold its ground against such opponents as foxes, weasels, ferrets, and rats. From the earliest days until modern time, terriers have exhibited courage that belies their moderate size. Pound for pound, there are few breeds that can match the energy, bravery, and stamina of a terrier.

There are more than twenty breeds that formally comprise the Terrier Group, as defined by the American Kennel Club (AKC). There are a number of other breeds that have been assigned to the Toy, Working, and Nonsporting Groups that stem from these early strains of "earthe dogges," as terriers were formerly known.

Terriers have evolved into a wide variety of types, and ears, tails, and coats have been further modified by human intervention. Typical ear configurations include: (1) folded, (2) cropped, (3) prick, and (4) pendulous.

Most terriers were originally kept by peasants and members of the working class, not as pets but as working dogs to control the pest population. Terriers of all varieties proved to be tireless "ratters" with an innate desire to please and serve their masters. Such loyalty and enthusiasm in time earned such dogs a place in the home as companions as well.

The British Isles are generally regarded as the homeland of most of today's terrier breeds. Because of Britain's varied terrain, terrier breeders were forced to breed their dogs selectively to adapt to the local conditions. Two main groups eventually were established: long-legged and short-legged terriers. The long-legged varieties are generally regarded as the "English" type, with smooth coats, rectangular heads, and erect tails. The short-legged varieties, or the "Scottish" type, typically have a rough coat, a larger head, and a low-slung posture.

Over the years other terrier breeds that did not fit these two classifications also emerged. Some larger, powerfully built terriers were developed to function primarily as fighting breeds in a "sport" long since banned in Britain and the United States. The Staffordshire bull terrier and the American Staffordshire terrier (often referred to as the American pit bull terrier) stem from these lines.

The modern day breeds that trace back to a terrier heritage are:

Airedale terrier
American Staffordshire terrier
Australian terrier
Bedlington terrier
Border terrier
Boston terrier
bull terrier
cairn terrier
Dandie Dinmont terrier
fox terrier, smooth, wire, and toy
Irish terrier
Kerry blue terrier
Lakeland terrier
Manchester terrier, standard and toy
Norfolk terrier
Norwich terrier
schnauzer, standard, giant, and miniature
Scottish terrier
Sealyham terrier
silky terrier
Skye terrier
soft-coated wheaten terrier
Staffordshire bull terrier
Welsh terrier
West Highland white terrier
Yorkshire terrier

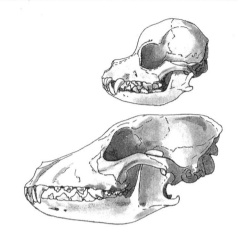

Terrier skull types include the compact variety found in such English breeds as the Border terrier (top), and the more elongated variety found in the Scottish terrier (bottom).

An elegantly groomed Yorkshire terrier proudly displays her new puppy (top). A silky, one of the two terrier breeds that originated in Australia (bottom).

Considerations Before You Buy

Is a Terrier the Right Breed for You?

Selecting a terrier puppy requires more than a decision of which dog or breed is "best." Prospective owners must also take the time to evaluate their lifestyle and the suitability of a dog, specifically a terrier, in their home.

A terrier is an active, often headstrong dog. A good owner must commit to training the dog thoroughly in the basic commands and supplying it with daily love, attention, adequate housing, and an outlet for its energy. Many terrier breeds require a considerable amount of grooming and regular exercise. An owner must make a commitment for the life span of the dog to fulfill its needs, including daily walks for approximately the next 10 to 15 years.

Various types of terriers: an Airedale, a Norwich, and a Boston.

A Norwich and a Norfolk terrier (top left). Norfolk terriers (top right, bottom right). A Norwich terrier (bottom left).

Some terriers do not do well in households with small children or other pets. Be sure the breed you select is appropriate for all members of your family. Make certain that a terrier puppy will be welcomed by everyone in the family. Despite good intentions, family members who did not want a dog around may suddenly become "allergic" to it or find it a nuisance. Such situations generally spell disaster for the dog, so think carefully and discuss this acquisition with all involved.

Tea time for some pals.

If you do not have a lot of time to devote to a terrier puppy, you may want to consider an older dog. Puppies require much attention and training while young. They need frequent walks and access to the outside during the housebreaking process. A well-trained older dog may be more appropriate for those who cannot be at home during long stretches of time.

Finally, consider the cost of keeping a terrier. Aside from the initial purchase price, an owner must supply routine veterinary care and an adequate, nutritious diet. In addition, many terrier breeds need regular professional grooming. Such costs are considerable and constant throughout the dog's life.

Considerations Before You Buy

Purchasing Your Terrier

Once you have resolved that a terrier really is the dog for you, you must decide what type you are looking for in order to find the best source for your dog. Are you looking for a show competitor or a companion? If you are looking for a pet, your resources are many. If you are searching for a potential winner in competitive contests, you need to do some research and make a careful selection.

Selecting a puppy destined to be a show dog is a gamble. Most puppies are purchased at eight to ten weeks of age—a time when little of the mature physique can be accurately evaluated. Most terriers develop rather slowly, often reaching physical maturity and acquiring their adult coloring at 24 months or later. Selections made prior to this are guesses at best; you can only base your choice upon pedigree and the breeders' knowledge of their dogs. If possible, hold off purchasing a show prospect until it is *at least* four to six months of age, when a slightly more reliable evaluation can be made. Puppies deemed "show quality" generally demand a hefty purchase price.

There are many outlets for those seeking a dog for a companion. Breeders of show dogs should also be able to supply "pet-quality" dogs. Potential champions are rare, and most litters contain well-bred terriers that are not competitive quality because of some minor fault. Such puppies are often very safe bets, as the pedigrees of both dam (female dog) and sire (male dog) are known and the puppies have been raised during the formative stages by knowledgeable people. The price of such puppies, reflecting their heritage and the care they have been given, will generally range from several hundred dollars up.

Pet terriers can also be purchased from pet stores or neighborhood litters. If you consider a pet-store dog, I suggest that you investigate from where the puppy was purchased and get as much

In dog show competition each entry vies to be selected as the dog that best represents the ideal image of the breed as defined by the official standard.

information as possible on its initial care. Many pet shops have been branded as selling inferior, often unhealthy puppies purchased from the "puppy mills" of midwestern America where the animals are mass-produced from whatever breeding stock is at hand. This is not always the case, however. Small local kennels often supply respectable pet stores. Research should quickly tell you about the pet-store puppy's beginnings. Terriers bought from pet shops are often priced the same as pet-quality dogs available at established kennels, so bear this in mind.

Neighborhood litters are a popular source for pet terriers at a reasonable price. Before you buy you should verify that both the mother and father are registered purebreds and that your puppy's litter is registered or eligible for registration with the American Kennel Club. Without such confirmation you cannot be assured that you are buying a purebred terrier and the price should reflect this. When buying a puppy that is the offspring of totally unrelated parents (usually the case with random breedings), you will rarely buy a future conformation champion. A puppy from a neighborhood litter can, however, still be a fine representative of its breed.

To help in your search, the names and addresses of local and national terrier organizations can be obtained by writing to the American Kennel Club, 51 Madison Avenue, New York, New York 10010. Another informative source is their monthly publication, *Purebred Dogs: American Kennel Gazette,* which contains a breed column, a list of advertising kennels, information on all aspects of dog care, and upcoming show and trial listings.

What to Look for in a Terrier Puppy

Your terrier puppy should be carefully evaluated for general health and essential breed characteristics. Before you inspect your potential puppy, look closely at the environment in which it was raised. The kennel or living quarters should be neat, clean, and free from parasites. Try to see the litter as a whole. Choosing a good puppy from a poor litter is risky.

Familiarize yourself with the breed standard and use it as a guideline. It is preferable that you see both dam and sire to get a general impression of the size and type of stock from which your puppy stems. In many cases only the dam is available, but she partially indicates whether the litter traces to healthy beginnings. Remember, however, that the dam may appear run-down after the rigors of whelping and nursing a litter. In this case, ask to see a prepregnancy picture. If your puppy's litter is the result of a repeat mating, ask to see some of the maturing dogs from the previous litter or for the name and phone number of an owner. This is especially important when purchasing a show prospect.

In evaluating an eight-week-old puppy, note first its overall appearance. Remember that most of the dog's growth will take place during the first 12 months and that different skeletal areas grow at different rates. A dog at this early stage is apt to

appear slightly out of balance. However, a puppy should be clean, pleasant smelling, and plump. Bloating, however, can indicate worm infestation. The eyes should be clear and without discharge and the ears should be pink inside. In several terrier breeds the puppy's coat is not even close to its mature color, so bear this in mind.

The puppy should be full of enthusiasm and should not shy away too easily. To test this, gently remove it from its littermates and see if it still continues to wag its tail or show interest in play. Timidity is not typical of a terrier.

What Age Puppy Is Best?

Most puppies are purchased at eight to ten weeks of age, when they are developmentally in what is known as the "human socialization period." This period, which lasts only until the puppy is about three months old, is the best time in a dog's life for it to learn to live with humans.

Experts recommend that a puppy be separated from its dam and littermates and placed in a home during the eighth week of life because it is forming permanent bonds at this time. If allowed to remain with the litter, the primary bond will be to dogs rather than humans, which is a hindrance to the human-dog relationship. Conversely, it is also important that a puppy not be removed from the litter before eight weeks—during the "canine socialization period"—because this period with dam and littermates is essential to produce a dog that can get along with other animals. Terriers are especially prone to aggressive behavior toward other dogs. If removed from the litter too early, the puppy may not have fully learned the lessons of animal socialization; the result is likely to be an adult dog that reacts too aggressively or too submissively when it meets another dog. Such dogs often become fighters or "fear biters" who are so easily upset that they lash out at other dogs and people. Puppies born in the so-called "puppy mills" are often taken from their litters at six or seven weeks of age so that they can arrive in pet stores at the most adorable age — eight weeks. While this gets the puppies to the market at their most "salable" time, it can have dire effects on the normal socialization process.

If you cannot arrange to pick up your puppy at approximately eight or nine weeks of age, ask that it begin to have foster human care rather than be left with the litter until you can bring it home.

The Purchase Agreement

Once you have selected your puppy and settled with the breeder on a purchase price, make it official by putting the terms of the deal in writing. This often prevents later difficulty if the dog proves unacceptable for health reasons or if you fail to receive all the documents promised you. The breeder should allow the new owner a set number of days to return the puppy if it fails a health examination by the new owner's veterinarian. Get this condition in writing. Such an agreement should also clarify whether an ill dog will be replaced or if the purchase price will be refunded.

At the time of sale, the breeder should supply you with the puppy's American Kennel Club registration application, most of which is filled out by the breeder. This application includes the names and AKC numbers of the sire and dam, information on the puppy's litter, and the name and address of the puppy's new owner. The new owner completes the form by listing two possible names for the puppy, signing, and enclosing the proper fee. If all is in order, the paperwork should take about three to four weeks to process. If the breeder has been following proper procedure (be wary of those who have not), the puppy's litter should have been registered with the AKC at birth. The breeder thus receives AKC applications prior to any sale. If the applications are not available, be sure to get from the breeder a signed bill of sale stating the breed, sex, and color of the puppy; the date of birth;

and the registered names of the sire and dam, with numbers, if available. This information is vital should you need to contact the American Kennel Club in search of "missing" papers.

In Junior Showmanship young exhibitors learn the skill of presenting their dogs for judging.

If you are buying a puppy from a show-oriented kennel, you may find that the breeder poses some special conditions. In the case of a top-quality animal, the breeder may stipulate terms concerning future mating of the dog. (But, quite honestly, in most cases a breeder would not let go of what looks like a potential top contender.) With pet-quality puppies from such kennels the breeder may agree to sell the dog only if the new owner agrees not to breed it. In the case of a puppy carrying a disqualifying fault, the breeder may even withhold the puppy's registration papers until proof is supplied that the dog has been neutered. The breeder may offer an attractive selling price to close such a deal. In this way the breeder is trying to eliminate faulty, genetically inferior animals from passing along their faults to future generations. Such dogs can still make fine pets.

Keeping and Caring for Your Terrier

A New Puppy In The Home

While leaving the security of its dam and litter-mates can be upsetting for a dog, most terriers make the transition with great ease. With few exceptions, terriers are very people-oriented and they adapt well to the "human pack." Many become intensely loyal and protective of their masters.

Equipment and Supplies
An owner can ease the transition by preparing ahead for the new puppy's arrival. Basic supplies to have on hand are: water and food bowls, food designed specifically for a puppy (preferably the food it has already been eating), a bed or crate, puppy-size collar and leash, grooming tools particular to your chosen terrier breed, and some safe chew toys.

The Earliest Lessons
The first few days in your home are an extremely important time, during which the dog will absorb a lot of information not only about its new territory but also about how you feel about the newcomer. A conscientious owner wants only positive experiences to get imprinted in the dog's mind and strives to make these early days as stress-free as possible.

The puppy's first few weeks in a new home should be devoted to mastering the lessons of living among humans. The dog will learn that there are pros and cons. The pros are the fun and the affection; the cons are the corrections. A puppy certainly can understand some simple lessons and corrections. A puppy's dam has already shown it that there are rules and limits on behavior. A considerable amount of learning takes place while the puppy is quite young, and these lessons are permanently remembered. At this point, the puppy should not have developed any bad habits, so this is a good time to begin teaching basic manners. Through careful moni-toring and positive corrections an owner can constructively shape the behavior of the future adult terrier.

The First Day

It is best to pick up the puppy from its breeder when you have several vacation days or a long weekend to familiarize the dog with its new home. It would be unfortunate to pick up a puppy one day and leave it alone the next while you go off to work or school; the puppy may feel abandoned and then have great difficulty feeling secure in its new home.

Be sure to treat the puppy gently and to speak to it in soft tones. Even though terrier puppies are pretty rough-and-tumble, roughhousing is not appropriate in the first few days in a new home. Play should be calm and filled with lots of affection and praise. The dog will need to be reassured, comforted, and encouraged during this trying period. Immediately upon arrival in the home show it where its food and water bowls are located, and take it to the elimination area. Once it has received the basic tour, let the dog roam and explore its new environment on its own, while you, of course, supervise from a distance. Allow the puppy to set the pace, and remember that frequent rest periods are necessary.

It will need its own sleeping area, preferably a sleeping box or crate (see more on crates in "Housebreaking" page 24). The puppy will return to this "den" for all sleeping periods. Allow the puppy to sniff and investigate this area soon after arriving in the home and return the dog to this sleeping area whenever it shows signs of tiring. Having a place of its own will instill in the puppy a sense of belonging and security during a very upsetting time. Until reliably housetrained, a puppy should be confined whenever it is not being directly supervised.

During the first few days try not to overstimulate the puppy. One way to go easy on the dog is to introduce only the members of the immediate family; save the neighbors for a few days later.

If there are other pets in the home, if possible hold off on letting them meet until the puppy has had a little time to get its bearings. When they meet, make sure all participants are strictly supervised. Praise the animals highly if they remain peaceable toward each other. If any of the animals react negatively, correct improper behavior with a stern warning and remove offenders from the area. Try again at regular intervals. A new puppy is often seen as a rival by established household pets, but this usually eases up as each animal takes its place in the pecking order that animals establish for themselves. Adult male terriers are often quite aggressive toward other dogs, especially other adult males, but they usually react less aggressively toward puppies. Things usually get better with time.

When introducing a terrier to a cat, remember that these two species do not share a common body language and they will probably not react favorably. This is especially true if either or both of the animals is an adult. If a dog has been raised since a puppy with cats, it will generally be peaceable toward cats throughout its life. If, however, an adult terrier is suddenly asked to tolerate a cat, you are asking for trouble.

It is inadvisable to keep as household pets any of the small animals that are the natural prey of terriers. This includes hamsters, mice, guinea pigs, and even rabbits. Should they get out of their cages, by natural instinct the terrier would go after them aggressively and destroy them. Even the best trained terrier cannot be relied upon to go against its instinct to kill rodents and small predators.

Owners should take pains to avoid jealousy and resentment by showing equal amounts of affection toward all pets in the home. It is easy to get caught up in making the new puppy feel at home, while the old-timers are neglected. This makes for hard feelings.

The First Night

Most puppies will whimper or cry during the first few nights and during periods of short separation. It is important to remember that the experience of the first few nights will shape the course of the nights to come, so do not be too soft-hearted and allow the puppy to sleep with you unless you plan on allowing this in the future. Consistency is at the heart of all training, and you cannot allow the puppy to do something this week that is forbidden the next. The new puppy is justifiably upset and you should do your best to comfort it. Place the dog in its sleeping area, pet it, talk soothingly, and then retire. If the puppy carries on desperately, return to it and comfort it again, but do not stay too long. Do not remove it from the sleeping area or pick it up, as this is reinforcement to the dog that if it howls long enough you will come and get it. You may want to help ease its tension by playing some soft, soothing music or by placing a hot water bottle under its blanket to imitate the mother's warmth. These measures should relieve the dog enough for it to fall asleep. The amount of attention needed should decline each night as the puppy gets used to the process.

Daytime Care

A puppy requires almost constant attention and should not be expected to stay by itself for more than short periods before it is physically mature enough and adjusted to its role in the household. A puppy that is left alone for great lengths of time will feel abandoned. This insecurity will adversely affect the way it bonds with its master, in particular, and possibly with all humans. A lonely puppy often becomes a maladjusted adult dog, and little can be done later to counteract a poor beginning. The result is often a high-strung dog with undesirable habits, such as tension chewing or scratching.

If you must go out for an extended length of time, take the dog with you. If this is impossible, try to leave the dog with someone (preferably someone it is acquainted with). Failing all else, arrange to have someone come to your home several times a day to socialize the puppy and attend to its exercise and elimination needs. Many school-age children will jump at the chance for such a fun part-time job. In many cities, there are professional "dog walkers" that can be hired to watch your dog during this critical period.

These extraordinary measures are important when a puppy or newly acquired dog is not mature enough to handle the physical and emotional stress of an extended separation. Things will improve, however, and early care and nurturing will go a long way to produce a happy, confident terrier adult.

Socialization

Local breed and obedience clubs often sponsor puppy socialization classes in which puppies are taught simple positive behaviors, such as how to walk on a leash, sit, or come. (See also pages 32–39.) These classes are not designed for formal obedience training, but rather as a nonstressful introduction to basic discipline and training techniques.

The course is aimed as much on teaching proper methods to the owner as it is focused on the puppy. For a modest fee, instructors outline

basic discipline and housetraining techniques, explain health and nutrition requirements, and clarify how a puppy learns and understands. This knowledge will enable the owner to establish a position of leadership and gain control over the puppy right from the start. Many novice owners do not understand that a dog expects a leader to behave in certain ways. If the dog does not receive the cues it expects from a leader, it will try to assume that position itself. Puppy socialization classes help produce more effective owners.

A pet door provides an easy way to give your terrier access to both the house and its fenced-in area outside.

The puppy benefits greatly from these socialization classes, as it learns not only vital lessons on life but is exposed to other people and dogs. By having some puppy-to-puppy socialization at an early age, the dog learns how to handle itself when around other animals. Terriers are, by instinct, slightly antagonistic when encountering another dog. Early socialization is vital to keeping this tendency under control, as the dog will need self-restraint when it meets other animals on the street or in the veterinarian's office. Having a game nature is no excuse for unruly behavior.

This early indoctrination will also instill a sense of accomplishment and self-confidence in the dog, as well as a positive attitude toward training. Puppy socialization classes are highly recommended for owners of terriers.

A fenced-in yard is essential to keep your terrier from roaming.

Outdoor Housing

While most terriers are hardy by nature and can function well when raised in an outdoor kennel, the majority of today's terriers are kept as house pets. Although frail or ill dogs should never be exposed to extremes of weather, terriers on the whole should be given plenty of access to the outdoors. They are earth dogs and need time in the yard to express their instincts by digging in the dirt and exploring their environment.

Any dog that spends time outdoors requires proper protection from the elements. A proper-sized, well-constructed doghouse will provide adequate shelter against heat, cold, and dampness. The interior must be roomy enough to allow the dog to stretch out, but not too large to maintain warmth. A well-designed doghouse has a hinged top for ease of cleaning, and is well insulated and draftproof. The entrance should be just large enough to allow the dog to enter easily.

During the summer the house must be placed in a shaded area, while a sunny spot is best during cold periods. If possible, have the house sitting on a solid foundation other than earth. One possibility is to place the house on blocks to stand several inches off the ground. This allows air to flow underneath and prevents direct contact with the soil.

A well-constructed dog house allows the dog some freedom of movement, is draft-free, and can be easily cleaned.

Two alert terriers awaiting their master's command: an Australian terrier (top); a Border terrier (bottom).

Keeping and Caring for Your Terrier

Any area where a terrier is allowed to roam freely should be properly fenced. As terriers are avid diggers, the fence must be deeply set to thwart the dog's ability to tunnel under it and escape. The doghouse should of course be positioned so that the dog cannot climb upon it and use it to jump over the fence.

This type of run provides a terrier with a place to exercise and shelter from the elements. The fence must be deeply set to thwart attempts to tunnel under it.

Traveling with Your Terrier

Terriers are very people-oriented and will usually prefer to accompany you than to stay home alone. From the time the dog is a puppy you should accustom it to riding in the car. You can begin with short trips, such as local errands, and increase from there. The dog should always be

The cairn terrier, which originated on the British Isle of Skye (top). The Sealyham is of Welsh origin (bottom).

placed in the back seat, and it should be lying down or in its crate when the car is in motion. Harnesses are available from dog specialty shops that allow you to loosely tether the dog to the seat belt attachment for safety.

In mild weather keep the car windows open approximately two inches during the ride to improve air circulation. Never allow the dog to hang its head out the window while the car is in motion, as this can result in eye, ear, and throat injuries.

During hot periods, provide the dog with a small amount of water at regular intervals to prevent dehydration when traveling without air conditioning. *Never leave a dog unattended in a parked car during the heat of the day.* Even with the windows slightly lowered, the internal temperature of the car can soar in just minutes and prove fatal to the trapped dog.

For trips of more than one hour, it is best not to feed the dog before leaving to avoid bouts with motion sickness. If your dog is prone to vomiting in the car and you are planning an extended ride, consult your veterinarian about medications to help alleviate the dog's nausea. Most dogs outgrow this tendency toward motion sickness as they get more accustomed to car trips. On long trips, plan to stop every two hours to allow the dog to relieve itself and get some exercise. It is especially important to remember to keep the dog on leash during these stops in unfamiliar terrain, where your terrier may bolt and get lost.

If your trip requires overnight lodging, be sure to carefully plan where you will be staying and make advance reservations, as many facilities will not allow dogs. Travel guides and your local automobile club may be able to supply you with a useful list of places that will allow animals.

Whenever traveling with a dog, take along an adequate supply of the dog's normal food. This helps reduce the chance of digestive upset from a sudden new diet. When the animal is already faced with so many new experiences, having a reliable supply of food is a good preventive measure.

Keeping and Caring for Your Terrier

A special restraint leash can be placed on the dog to keep it secure when riding in the car.

If you are unable to bring your dog with you on your travels, you will need to find good accommodations for your pet while you are away. The best solution is to have as caretaker someone the dog is familiar with. If this is not possible, you have several options to consider. The breeder from whom you purchased the dog may be in a position to board it temporarily; the pluses of this are the familiarity the breeder would have with the individual dog and the particular requirements and traits of the breed.

Commercial kennels routinely offer boarding services. Most are well run, clean, and attentive to the dog's basic needs. Before leaving your dog at a kennel, however, be sure to visit it and view the facility. If all seems in order, check that it is accredited by the American Boarding Kennel Association (ABKA). A list of approved kennels in your area can be obtained by writing the ABKA at 4575 Galley Road, Suite 400A, Colorado Springs, Colorado 80915. Once a kennel has been selected, leave enough of the dog's normal food to last until your return.

Air travel for animals has improved greatly in the last few years; progressive legislation requires all animals to be shielded from extremes of temperature. In recent times, traveling in airplanes has become commonplace for show dogs and for planned matings that involve partners from various areas of the country. Various precautions are worth noting, however.

Most airlines will, for an additional charge, furnish owners with a suitable crate for shipping a dog, if they do not own one themselves. Each airline has its own boarding procedures, so be sure to check prior to departure time for instruction on how to proceed. Arrange to have a supply of the dog's normal food delivered with the dog upon arrival.

Be very thorough in marking the shipping crate. Clearly mark the outside of the container with "Live Animal" and the dog's name, as well as the name, address, and phone number of both the sender and the recipient. Include another copy of this information *in the crate* with the dog.

For added comfort, place a blanket at the bottom of the crate. If permitted, one soft chew toy may be enclosed to help alleviate tension and boredom during the trip. Be sure to exercise the dog just before placing it in the container, and stay with it for as long as possible before loading on the plane.

Before you leave the airport, verify with airline officials that the dog has, indeed, been loaded aboard the plane. This cargo is more than a piece of luggage—and since airlines have been known to misplace luggage, make many people connected with the flight aware of the dog's presence and its intended destination. You cannot be too careful when leaving your terrier in someone else's care.

Training Your Terrier

Terriers are a highly energetic, intelligent lot. Left unchecked, these characteristics could lead the dog charging down the wrong behavioral path. Properly channeled, these same traits can help produce a well-mannered, enthusiastic, reliable companion. Most terriers exhibit a lot of spunk, independence, and a zest for life. This must be tempered and guided by a large dose of discipline, right from the start.

When it is quite young, a dog learns its first lessons on manners from its mother. The mother is the undisputed leader and maintains her position by swift discipline whenever a puppy gets out of line. She admonishes her young by using a progression of techniques, starting with low, guttural growls, then (if needed) a swat of the paw, and (if really pushed) a quick shake of the offender's neck. Rarely is any further action required. The mother reacts fairly, unemotionally, and consistently, and the puppies respect her authority. She is the boss—the "alpha figure."

This pattern of discipline traces back to earliest times when dogs roamed in packs. From the pack, one leader emerged; all other pack members then assumed various ranks behind the leader. The leader's authority would occasionally be challenged by the underlings, many of whom competed for independence and power. Even today every dog assumes it is "top dog" until proven otherwise (I call this the "leader of the pack syndrome"). A leader must clearly show any upstart by swift reprimand that its place is not at the head of the pack. Once all pack members submit to the leader's authority, they follow and cooperate fully.

This heritage of pack behavior is still significant today and must be dealt with in your terrier's training. You must take over the leadership position vacated by the puppy's mother—by becoming the new alpha figure. Your dog must also be taught to be respectful of all humans, not only the alpha. While this might sound harsh, it really isn't. The owner must simply learn to discipline the dog in a manner it understands and respects. Screaming, brutalizing, whining, or pleading will not make your dog feel compelled to respond. A worthy leader does not act that way. Generally all that is needed is a firm vocal reprimand (in a low tone, similar to a dog's warning growl), a stern look, and perhaps a shake of neck. Hitting and yelling are counterproductive actions that do little except confuse the dog and interfere with the human-dog bond. A leader corrects *every* misdeed immediately, firmly, fairly, and consistently. Letting some misdeeds go uncorrected will undermine a leader's authority.

Basic obedience training is not a spirit-breaking process but rather a confidence-building one. Training teaches the dog the rules of proper behavior in the home, in public, and in the presence of other animals. To get a spirited, sometimes willful terrier to obey commands, the dog must be shown that compliance brings rewards (petting, praise), while disobedience brings disadvantages (scolding and your displeasure). You will find that

If you want your terrier to stay off the furniture, it must be *consistently* told "No!" from early on.

your terrier loves to please you, adores praise and affection, and does not resent correction or punishment when it is due.

Setting the limits of your dog's actions is your responsibility. The dog must be shown clearly and consistently what is acceptable behavior and what is not. You can't let Rocco share your popcorn and sit on the sofa at night and scold him the next morning for napping there or trying to taste your cheese Danish. You are giving the dog mixed signals. Unvarying and repeated corrections are necessary for your dog to understand your rules and learn to obey. Most behavioral problems arise from poor teachers rather than poor learners. Trainers must be unmistakably clear about what is expected and how things are to be done and must be prepared to show the dog how to react, correct the dog's mistakes, show the procedure again, and praise each little success. Dogs learn by repeated simple patterns of correction and praise, and each dog learns at its own pace.

Training the Terrier Puppy

The first steps to a well-mannered terrier should be taken when the puppy arrives in the new owner's home. Of course, an eight-week-old puppy cannot understand or respond to formal commands, but it can learn that some things please the master and result in a pleasurable experience and some things don't. All training should enforce the idea that learning not only is fun but also brings positive responses from the owner. Learning need not be unpleasant.

Nothing inspires a desire to learn more than success. Make the first training goals simple. An easily accomplished task is to get the dog to respond to its name. Simply use the name whenever dealing with the dog, and offer high praise when it reacts properly. This gives the dog a quick success

and the rewards of a proper response. Terriers thrive on positive reinforcement and quickly form a lifelong bond to their masters who treated them lovingly in the early weeks of life.

With each little training success your terrier will gain confidence both in itself and in you. The dog learns that you respond positively when it reacts in a certain manner to certain situations. If it acts otherwise, it is corrected. This consistent praise/correction pattern lays the foundation for learning. Mistakes will be made, but with precise guidelines the dog learns what it may and may not do. Formal training is simply teaching the dog that certain actions or commands require certain reactions.

Housebreaking

Housebreaking is the puppy's first real challenge. If handled properly, training should not be a painful experience for owner or pet. Since terriers take to this task naturally, it should be accomplished rather quickly.

The owner must first understand *when* the puppy will need to eliminate: after eating, after waking, after strenuous play, first thing in the morning, last thing at night. These are definite times. There will also be in-between times. The puppy will usually give cues that indicate the need to eliminate, such as looking uneasy, sniffing, and walking in circles as if searching for something. Until three to six months of age a puppy has very limited control of its bladder and cannot physically "hold it." Such control will be mastered later.

The key to housebreaking success is being an attentive owner: knowing when the puppy will need to eliminate, monitoring its physical signs, getting the puppy out quickly, and praising each little success.

Training Your Terrier

Terriers, like all dogs, retain a pack instinct. One of the pack traits is the desire to keep the "den" area clean. This is generally instilled in the dog by its mother, who makes it quite clear from an early age that she will not tolerate soiling of the sleeping area. Puppies learn quickly to eliminate away from the sleeping quarters or suffer a motherly correction. By the time your puppy reaches your home, it probably already knows that some areas are acceptable for elimination and others are not. This applies to puppies that were raised by their dams until weaning. The owner must build on this early indoctrination.

Always remember that housebreaking is a learning process and mistakes are inevitable. Since most "accidents" are not incidents of willful misbehavior, they should be dealt with calmly. Until the puppy truly understands the proper procedure, there should be no punishment for mistakes—just a correction and an indication of what proper behavior is. React in a manner the puppy can understand (that is, react as its dam would). Correct swiftly, firmly, fairly. Show displeasure by sternly saying, "No!" and giving the dog an angry look. Show the dog the proper procedure by taking it to the correct elimination area and lavishly praising it. *Never* hit the puppy or rub its nose in its excrement. Such confusing and humiliating acts are damaging not only to the housebreaking process but also to the bond you are trying to establish with your dog.

As your terrier matures, it will gain control of its bodily functions, but until that time, there will be accidents. When you discover an unwanted deposit, *do not overreact*. Let the dog know you are displeased, but you must also let it know exactly what you are displeased about. You must help the dog make a connection between the excrement on the floor and your attitude. Don't assume by your dog's "guilty" behavior that it knows why you are upset. When the dog skulks away to a far corner, tail between legs, it

is exhibiting a fear reaction, not a guilty conscience. Calmly go to the dog and lead it to the spot. Have the dog look at the excrement. Point at it and scold the dog in a low, almost growling tone. Immediately remove the dog to the proper elimination area. If this is a continuing problem, you may want to confine the dog to its sleeping quarters for a short "time out" once you bring it back into the house.

Remember, screaming, brutalizing, and carrying on over housebreaking mistakes accomplish nothing productive. Such actions confuse and frighten the dog, and will not even reinforce the owner's position as leader. Correcting and banishing are the actions of a leader; ranting and physically abusing an animal are not actions a dog will respect.

When you are faced with a cleanup, wash the area with a solution designed to remove excrement odors (available from veterinarians and pet shops) or with a soapy solution containing a little vinegar. Do not use an ammonia-based cleaner, as this will reattract the dog to the spot rather than repel it.

Establish a routine from the first day the puppy is in your house. A very young puppy should be taken out almost hourly during waking hours and given a chance to eliminate. Giving the dog this much attention may seem like a burden, but things get better and it is worth it in the end. Over time, the number of trips outside will be reduced to just a few a day at maturity. Patience is of the utmost importance. A puppy that is rushed and harshly punished during this vital stage of training will often become a chronic soiler as an adult.

A "quick fix" that must be avoided is the tendency to just open the door and let the dog go out by itself. A puppy is easily distracted and may spend its time outside investigating the environment rather than eliminating. Once inside, the puppy may then relieve itself, incurring the wrath

Training Your Terrier

of the owner who "just took the dog out." Always accompany the dog during the training period. A puppy needs instruction and, most of all, praise. Praise is the most effective training tool the owner has, and it should be used lavishly.

Until the dog is reliably housebroken, limit its access to unsupervised areas of the household. If given the run of the house, it will regard the entire house as its playground. A puppy does not want to soil its den, but it does not regard its playground as highly. Establish an area that will serve as the sleeping quarters and an area for elimination. If possible, have this elimination area outside, rather than a papered area in the house (see Paper Training page 27). The intermediate paper stage is necessary only if the owner cannot be present in the home for long stretches of time during the training process. Bring the puppy to the same elimination spot each time it shows signs of needing to go, and praise *every* success. Correct each mistake firmly but fairly, and immediately return the puppy to the correct spot. Repetition, correction, and praise form the backbone of the housebreaking process.

You can help your own cause by following a schedule for feeding the puppy, feeding the prescribed amount (no snacks), and removing the water bowl at night. These easy steps help to regulate the dog's elimination needs and help you predict when the dog will need to go out.

When not under direct supervision, the puppy should be confined to a limited area of the household or crated. Choose a small, uncarpeted area and block off all escape routes. A mesh baby gate will do well for most terrier breeds, but may not be high enough for some of the larger, more nimble breeds, such as the Airedale.

Crates

Crates are effective training tools, and should not be regarded as prisons. Crating a puppy is the most efficient method of housebreaking, and is not cruel or inhumane. As pack animals, dogs have an inborn desire for the security of a den. Most dogs take quite easily to the crate, and instinctively try to keep this den area clean by not eliminating in it.

Crates can be purchased from pet shops and dog supply stores. They are most often constructed of heavy-duty plastic or wire mesh. A crate must be large enough for the dog to sit or lie down comfortably.

When used together with a regular schedule of walks and feeding, the crate is a very valuable tool. Of course, it should not be abused. A puppy will be forced to relieve itself if confined for too long a stretch of time. This defeats the purpose of the crate. The owner must take the dog to its proper elimination area at regular intervals and offer enthusiastic approval there each time it relieves itself. Terriers, which thrive on praise, will soon make the connection between eliminating in this area and admiration from its owner. This is the big breakthrough!

A growing puppy has many requirements. It must be fed at least three times a day (7:00 A.M., 12:00 noon, and 5:00 P.M. are common schedules) and walked very frequently. The puppy can be crated for brief periods between the walks. It is often helpful to remain in the room with the puppy during the first few cratings. Pay no attention to the dog unless there are signs of distress. Terriers are very intuitive. If they sense anxiety in their owner's behavior they may either use this to their advantage (they are quite bright and can be manipulative); on the other hand, they may feel there really *is* something to be feared (since the master is obviously upset) and become unnerved by the crating experience. Many people find this hard to believe, but most dogs enjoy their crates and regard it as a comforting place to rest and relax. While in the crate, the dog will usually sleep.

The first cratings should last only five to ten minutes. This time can be increased gradually over the next few weeks. During the day, puppies under 12 weeks of age may remain in the crate for up to one hour; puppies 12 to 16 weeks of age may be crated for up to two hours; older puppies may stay a maximum of three to four hours in a crate. The maximum time allowed in the crate, which will vary from dog to dog, depends on the dog's age and its elimination requirements. After the initial training period, dogs of all ages can be crated overnight.

The location of the crate is important. It should be placed out of the direct line of household traffic, but not somewhere that will make the dog feel totally isolated. A blanket or towel can be placed on the bottom of the crate for additional comfort, and the dog should be permitted a chew toy or bone. Do not place bowls of food or water in the crate, however.

Once the dog is fully housebroken, the need for the crate is generally gone, but many dogs enjoy having a "den" and will often return to an open crate for naps.

Paper Training

Paper training is the slowest method of housebreaking, but it is useful for those who cannot be with the puppy for long periods during the day. A puppy cannot be expected to "hold it" all day while its owner is at work. Paper training provides a reasonable alternative until the dog gets older.

Whenever you are not with the puppy, confine it to a limited space. This space should then be divided into three areas: the elimination area, the feeding area, and the sleeping or crate area. (Many people who paper train also leave the puppy an opened crate to use as a den during the day.) Place several layers of newspapers in the

elimination area, making sure that paper does not extend into the other two areas.

Familiarize the puppy with the elimination area by placing the dog on the paper each time you think it needs to eliminate and every time the dog seems agitated. Encourage the puppy with "Do your business," "Good dog on the paper," or some similar phrase that does not include the words "come," "sit," or "down," as these will be used later when basic obedience commands are being taught. Putting a small piece of previously urine-soiled paper on each fresh pile of paper will help to reattract the dog to the elimination spot. Whenever the dog uses the papers, praise it highly to let it know that this area is acceptable for elimination and that you are pleased when it goes there.

Most terriers are real "outdoors" dogs and will readily accept appropriate outside locations when they are mature. Gradually shrink the area covered with newspapers until it is quite small. You might even place some sheets of paper outside a few times to let the dog know that the new elimination spot is acceptable.

At approximately six to twelve months of age most dogs gain enough control to make it through the day. After every "accident-free" extended stay in the house, praise the dog for not soiling and immediately take it to the elimination area. Owners who work outside the home should make sure to walk the dog just before leaving and as soon as returning.

Waste Cleanup

It is up to the owner to clean up after a pet. In many cities the law requires an owner to remove the solid waste excreted by pets, and owners who do not comply face fines ranging from $25 to $250.

Cleaning up such waste not only rids the streets and public areas of offensive and unhealthful materials, but also proves that dog owners as a whole are responsible people. Without such care, apartment dwellers will find it increasingly difficult to find housing where their pets are accepted.

The cleanup process is really quite easy. Scoops made just for this purpose are available in most pet stores. Another method is to invert a plastic bag to cover your hand, pick up the waste using the bag as a shield, allow the waste to fall back into the bottom of the bag, and dispose of it in the nearest garbage container.

A terrier should never be allowed outside unsupervised, as it will surely roam.

Rules for the Trainer

When deciding when to begin formal training, let the puppy be your guide. It is useless and frustrating for all involved to begin training a puppy that cannot understand what you want of it. As a general rule, most terriers can begin command training at six to eight months of age. Concentration is the key. If the puppy consistently wanders off—physically or mentally—it is probably too young, so try again in a few weeks.

The first lessons should be short, no more than ten minutes, but they should be held regularly—twice daily if possible. Repeat all lessons frequently, but proceed very slowly. Stop as soon as the dog shows signs of having trouble concentrating. Boredom in the early stages can cause serious damage to the dog's acceptance of future training.

Training should be serious, but not tedious. While you do not want the puppy to think training is just great fun, you do not want it to be a drudge either. Learning can be a stress-producing experience for the dog, so encourage and reassure it frequently. Praise the dog for each minor success, but don't go overboard and get the dog so excited that it forgets what the purpose of the lesson is. Praise enough to inspire the dog to do well and earn more praise.

Commands should be made in an authoritative, but not scolding tone. Never whine or plead with the dog to get it to comply. Remember: you are the alpha figure! Issue the *same* command each time you request a certain action (not "Rocco, come" one time and "Come here, boy" the next). As a general rule, include the dog's name in any command that requires motion (heel, come) but omit it from the commands where the dog is to remain motionless (sit, down, stay). Similarly, give your terrier cues to what its response to a command will be by always stepping off with your *left* foot when the dog is to move out with you and with your *right* foot when you move away from the dog alone. These are some of the little things that have an unconscious effect on your dog's response.

Owners should understand that terriers are quite *sight sensitive,* and that this affects training. Terriers are instinctively attracted to any sudden movement—from the rustling of leaves to the movements of squirrels. These things alert all their senses and awaken instinctive drives to

Training Your Terrier

pursue the moving object. Terriers (especially males) are also aggressive toward any dogs they feel are in competition with them. Curbing such impulses is at best difficult. The preferred solution is to minimize the chance of such distractions during the initial stages of training by choosing a location that is distraction-free. The best site for early training is a well-lit, well-ventilated room that is as spacious and uncluttered as possible. Later, once the dog has shown that it has mastered basic techniques, adding distractions such as those found outdoors will test how well your terrier really knows and complies with the commands. If the dog forgets all that it has learned once it is asked to perform in a public spot, retreat to the more secluded training site for more drilling.

Remember, instincts will remain no matter how well a dog is trained. A well-trained dog, however, will be able to control its desires to a great extent. In time, it will perform reliably despite its inborn desire to chase after each unknown rustle in the underbrush.

Gain your terrier's attention before starting any lesson. Get the dog to make eye contact with you. This is the first step in inspiring interest, since an encouraging look from you creates in the dog anticipation and a desire to please.

Patience and consistency are the keys to effective training. Progress very slowly, as any action quickly learned is often quickly forgotten. Many repetitions of every action will be needed before the dog will really know how it is expected to respond. Give and enforce each command in the exact same way each time. The dog must then perform the required response fully—in the same way each time. Such drilling can test anyone's patience, but the repetitions eliminate confusion.

Verbal corrections are an instantaneous, "No!" You must then repeat the command and show the proper response once again. Repeat the command only when absolutely necessary; your

goal is to have the dog perform the action when given only one command.

Correct fairly and with love, not out of anger. The dog is probably making mistakes out of confusion, not willful misbehavior. Never shout or strike the dog. This will only make matters worse and possibly ruin the dog for further training. Since your terrier's enthusiasm is a great asset, you do not want to break its spirit. Emphasize the dog's successes rather than harp on its mistakes.

The severity of your correction must depend on the cause of your terrier's failure. Reprimanding a confused dog will be ineffective and in the long run will undermine the training process. Monitor the dog's body language for signs of distress or confusion (often reflected in a sunken posture and flatly drawn back ears). If confusion is evident, encourage your dog to succeed by breaking down the task into its simplest elements, leaving no chance of error. Praise, admire, celebrate! Taking such care should improve your terrier's chances of becoming a reliably trained pet, rather than a discouraged or disgruntled misfit.

Keep the lessons short and pleasant. If you quit while your dog is encouraged by its success and still eager, it will remain interested in learning more. Don't get carried away and push your terrier beyond its capabilities when things are going well. Continually asking the dog for "just one more" can lead to exhaustion and disinterest. If things aren't going well, don't give in to anger or frustration. Instead, revert to some simple action that the dog *can* succeed in, offer congratulations, and call it a day. Things will probably go more smoothly the next time.

Follow each lesson with a generous dose of approval and a pleasant activity, such as a walk or a game. Your terrier will appreciate the special attention and think of the training process as pleasurable.

Training Your Terrier

Breaking to Collar and Leash

The collar and leash (or lead) are the primary tools of training. When formal training is to begin, you will need to purchase a training or "choke" collar, which consists of a chain of metal links with a ring on each end. The training collar allows you to apply as much pressure as necessary to evoke the correct response by the dog. A light snap upwards is all that is needed to get the dog's attention and persuade it to correct its misdeed. The collar will momentarily tighten. Once the pressure is released, the collar will immediately loosen. Your dog will quickly learn that the upward tug and the resulting tightening signify your displeasure and that a correction is needed. Used properly the training collar is a valuable teaching aid. It should *never* be used inhumanely to inflict pain.

Choose a collar that is the appropriate size for your terrier—approximately the diameter of the head plus one or two inches. Overly large collars can be dangerous and are useless for quick corrections, so don't buy one the puppy will "grow into."

To form the training collar, slip the chain through one of the rings. Attach the leash to the free ring. When placing the collar on the dog's neck, be sure to slip it over the head so that the chain connecting to the free ring passes *over the top* of the neck. The rings should be positioned on the right side of the dog's neck, since the dog will always stand to your left during training. This positioning will allow the collar to relax instantly once the upward pressure is released. If placed improperly, the chain will remain taut around the neck too long and may injure your dog.

The training collar is to be worn *only* during lessons. Between lessons a lightweight nylon or leather collar can be worn continuously. Attach a medallion to this type of collar on which the

dog's name, your name, address, and phone number are listed. Any medical problems the dog may have should be inscribed as well. This tag can be invaluable should your terrier wander too far in search of a scent and become lost, or if it is involved in an accident.

An identification tag firmly attached to the collar is an important aid to retrieving a lost pet.

Once you have placed a collar on the dog, offer praise and let the dog wear it for a while to familiarize itself with the new weight. When the dog no longer balks at the feel of the collar, attach the training leash which is generally made of a light but sturdy webbed cloth, nylon, or leather. Correct with "No!" if the dog tries to chew the lead. If necessary, apply a slight upward tug to remove it from the dog's grasp. The leash is a symbol of authority, not a toy, so be firm. At first you can let the puppy drag the lead around to accustom it to this sudden weight, but closely monitor the dog's movement to make sure it does not get tangled or

hurt. A three-foot leash is best for training purposes, as it does not allow the dog to lag behind or
forge too far ahead.

The next step is to pick the lead up, but apply
no pressure. Follow the puppy around for several
minutes, and then let the pup know that it is time
to follow you. Slowly introduce the feel of the
upward tug. If the dog is frightened, reassure it,
but continue to apply firm pressure whenever it
wanders out of your control area. In a short time
you should be able to impress on the puppy that
the lead is a restraint that must be obeyed and
that the gentle tugs demand immediate attention.
Your terrier will soon be walking according to
your guidance. At this point, more formal instruction can begin.

The reel lead is an effective means for controlling the
amount of freedom your dog can have while strolling.

Tips for Training
Small or Toy Terriers

When training some of the smaller terriers, particularly the toy breeds (such as the Yorkshire or
silky terrier), you may have to modify some of
the basic training techniques to compensate for
the extreme difference in height between you and
your dog. A solid lead will aid the task. This is
basically a rod with a short expanse of leash at
its end. Held near your side it allows you to keep
your pet in proper position without having to
hunch over or clutch the several feet of leash that
would otherwise extend above the dog's head.

The solid lead is held in your right hand. In
your left hand hold a back scratcher or a similar
aid with which you can reach down and position
the dog. With this method you do not need to
bend continuously to correct the dog. You can
even use the back scratcher to scratch the dog's
back gently as a form of praise.

Training small dogs can be complicated (and
backbreaking). If your pet fails to progress, seek
the guidance of a trainer who can demonstrate
some of the more effective techniques for handling
small terriers. Through experimentation you
should be able to work out a method that is effective and comfortable for both you and your dog.

Remember, small or toy terriers are not to be
treated as fragile objects; they, too, need manners. Reinforce this concept from an early age:
do not carry them all the time and do not pamper
them. They will need additional consideration, of
course, and some added encouragement. In the
initial stages of training you could teach the dog
the fundamental commands by having it stand at
your side on a sturdy crate or other elevated surface. Once the dog is aware of what you want,
start the process over again with the dog positioned at your feet. Most dogs make the transition very smoothly.

Training Your Terrier

Encourage the dog to look up frequently, as eye contact is a vital part of a training program. You can accomplish this by making a short, staccato sound to get the dog's attention. If this fails, or if you feel silly making clucking noises (who could blame you?), you can gently tap the top of the dog's head with the training back scratcher or dangle a tempting tidbit or favorite toy in the air. Use your imagination and devise a system that works for you. The important point is that by making eye contact you are encouraging the dog to pay attention. Without the dog's attention, little progress will be made. After a few weeks, as the dog's familiarity and interest in the training process increases, you can stop the attention-getting maneuvers.

The Basic Commands

While only a dedicated few terriers and trainers are destined for high honors in the obedience trial rings, to be a trustworthy companion *every* terrier must master some basic commands. Two that are rather easily taught and learned are "no" and "off," which are more corrections than commands. The five basic commands that require more formal instruction are: "sit," "stay," "heel," "come," and "down." Upon learning to respond to these commands, your terrier will have earned a place in human company. Lacking this knowledge, the dog lacks restraint and should be kept on leash, tethered, or otherwise restricted from activities that require self-control and manners.

Sit

The "sit" is taught with the dog on leash, preferably indoors in a quiet location. At first the dog should be taught to sit at your left side, with its shoulders square to your leg. Later, once it has mastered this position, it can be taught to sit in front of you. Begin by placing the dog at your left side, while you hold the leash taut in your right hand, applying only enough upward pressure to keep the dog's head up. Command "Sit" while you firmly press your left hand on its rear to place it in the sitting position. Continue the upward pressure from the lead in your right hand and use the left to straighten your pet's position. Praise your dog as soon as it is properly positioned and release with "Good dog!" or an upward sweep of the left hand.

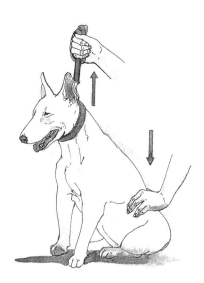

When teaching the "sit," apply upward pressure on the leash while pressing down on the hindquarters.

Training Your Terrier

Make the first few attempts quite short, thus not allowing the dog the opportunity to fall over on your leg or lie down. Gradually increase the required sitting time and be sure to praise the dog when it reaches the sit position—not as it breaks to get up. It must learn to associate the praise with the completion of the action. Should the dog attempt to move out of position, correct with "No!" and a slight jerk of the lead.

As the dog progresses, the amount of pressure you apply on the rear should be reduced and finally removed. Within a short time the sitting action will become habitual in response to the command. Once you reach this point you can begin training the "stay" and the "heel."

Stay

The "stay" command builds from the "sit." Do not attempt to teach the "stay" until your dog is reliably performing the "sit," as the dog will be required to remain in "sit" position until released.

Begin by placing the dog in a "sit." Keep some slight upward pressure on its neck from the leash in your right hand. As you command "Stay!" you must simultaneously move away from the dog using your *right* left and bring the palm of your left hand down toward its face, stopping short of touching its muzzle. Move only a short distance (about a foot at first) or the dog will try to follow you. Make sure that the hand signal is given at the same time that the command is given and the step taken. Retain eye contact, if possible. Repeat the command while maintaining the signal. The voice should be firm and authoritative. Do not expect the dog to stay for more than ten seconds or so at first; release your pet after small successes and offer praise.

When the dog breaks the "stay," return it immediately to the "sit" and repeat the whole procedure. Never let it get up by its own initiative without a swift correction, as the "stay" is a command that really tests a leader's authority. It

The "stay" is taught with the dog in the sit position. Move away from the dog as you command "Stay!" and signal with your palm toward the dog.

is normal but unacceptable for the dog to try to move toward you once it sees you move away, or to lie down once it sees that it is to remain where positioned. Be patient, correct each error, and do not expect immediate results. As you see improvement, extend the length of the time for the "stay" and the distance moved. The desired achievement is a dog that can be relied upon to remain in the "sit" position for at least several minutes. (The "down-stay," to be taught later, can and should be used daily as a more extended control measure.) This procedure requires the dog to maintain a lying down position for 30 minutes or more as a means of teaching the importance of discipline and enforcing your position as leader. It sounds impossible—and perhaps even cruel—but it really is a good method for taming a little of the terrier spunk.

Training Your Terrier

Heel

Most terriers will instinctively bolt forward when given the opportunity to investigate new or even familiar terrain. To train your dog to walk *with* you, at your pace, it will need to be taught to "heel." Heeling is no more than controlled walking—an act every dog should be expected to perform. The dog should always be on your left side, its chest preferably in line with your leg. The leash is held in your right hand and corrective pressure is applied by your left. Place the dog in a "sit" and begin by stepping off with your *left* foot, calling "Rocco, Heel!" as you move forward. Snap the leash as you give the command to start him forward, removing the pressure as he walks in "heel" position. Walk at a comfortable pace, applying pressure only if he surges ahead or lags behind. Make your snaps firm and repeat "Heel!" with each correction. Praise as soon as he responds, using a pleasant tone and "Good dog!"

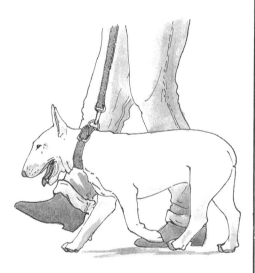

Every terrier should be taught to heel at its master's side when out for a walk.

Periodically repeat the praise—but don't overdo it—if the dog remains in proper position for extended lengths of time. As soon as you come to a halt, the dog is to sit. At first you will need to issue the "sit" command, and perhaps help the dog down, but as the dog progresses, the "sit" will become automatic when you stop, and no verbal cue will be needed.

Mastering the "Heel" will take time. As you encounter problems—such as your terrier's desire to surge ahead—you may want to resort to placing the dog in a "sit" to restore calm rather than continually snapping it back into proper position. Having the dog sit will allow it to succeed at a task with which it is already familiar, and thereby receive praise. This will keep you both at ease; the heeling practice can then continue rather than break down into confusion on the pet's part and anger on the trainer's. Once the dog has successfully completed the "sit," move it out again with "Rocco, Heel!" Offer praise if he comes and moves in the proper position. Stop him as soon as he misbehaves, giving a firm tug on the lead and a stern look.

It is imperative that you do not apply continuous pressure to the neck of a surging dog. The choke collar is effective as a sudden jarring that regains the dog's attention and brings about a correction. The snap on the lead must be swift and strong enough to get a response, but not so strong as to cause pain and possible injury. The choke should be used only when needed, should have an impact on the dog, and should be immediately released.

During the early attempts at heeling, keep the lessons short—no more than 10 to 15 minutes. As the dog becomes more adept—and no longer needs to be put in frequent corrective "sits"—extend the lessons as energy and interest (both yours and the dog's) may indicate. Even a well-trained terrier may react instinctively when it spots a small animal in the brush. Your patience will help your pet master self-restraint. So bear

Training Your Terrier

in mind that instinctive drives will often surface and deal with them as simple mistakes, not willful misbehavior.

Come

The "come" teaches a dog that it must return to its master at once, without hesitation. It is a command that will enforce your leadership position, as the dog must learn to stop whatever it is doing and return on command to its master's side. As terriers have a strong interest in whatever they happen to be doing, they are often reluctant to break their concentration to respond to the command. While they may quickly comprehend what the command means and what is expected, getting a reliable, wholehearted response will take time. Accept no less than a quick response every time, or the dog may choose not to obey at a crucial moment. The "come" command can be life-saving when used to remove the dog from danger.

You have already given your terrier informal training in this command. As a pup, it quickly learned to respond happily when called — probably in anticipation of play or food. Now the goal is to have your dog respond to your call regardless of the circumstances or how it perceives the situation (thereby overcoming the "what's in it for me?" syndrome).

Formal trailing for the "come" command should begin with a pleasant play period. Place the dog on a long leash (20 feet or more) and let it romp in the practice area. Maintain only minimal tension on the end of the lead. Once the dog is relaxed and concentrating on play or investigation of some nearby object, command "Rocco, come!" in a firm tone and snap the lead to start the dog in motion toward you. Offer praise as the dog *begins* to move toward you. Have him come directly to you and into a "sit." Should he fail to respond, give a sharp correction with the lead as you repeat "Come!" If necessary, repeat the command. You might have to reel the dog in by

slowly retracting the cord — but this is rarely required. Once the dog has completed the "come" and the companion command of "sit," release with "Good dog!" and let him move away from you again. Repeat the "come" command at various intervals. Should the dog fail to move immediately toward you, correct with a sharp snap on the lead.

Use of the "come" should not be overdone. Perform a few repetitions during all training lessons. Employ it also throughout the day when the dog's presence really is requested. *Never* command a dog to come and then punish it for an offense once it arrives at your side. It will associate coming with punishment. If you catch your dog in an inappropriate action, *go to it* and reprimand. If you call the dog and punish it when it arrives, you will almost certainly ruin your chances of having a dog that will instantly return to the "come."

Down

The "down" command is tied closely to the "sit" and "stay" commands. To teach the dog to lie down, place it first in a "sit" and kneel next to it. As you command "Down!" take hold of its front legs near the body, gently lift them from the floor, and lower the dog to the ground. Once down, command the dog to "Down, stay!" Follow this with "Good dog!" if it remains in the prone position. You may need to keep your left hand resting on its back to keep it from getting up. Pet your terrier briefly, release by motioning upward with your hand and gently tugging the lead, and return the dog to a "sit," on command, to begin again.

Do not make your dog remain in the down position too long at first, as the "down" concept needs to be reinforced to keep it clearly differentiated from the stay. Besure the dog remains lying on all fours for the short downs, not sprawled out on its side. The dog is to be alert on the down, not overly comfortable.

Practice the "down" several times each day. As the downward movement becomes more familiar, you will soon be able to stop guiding the legs down, so you can avoid kneeling down. During this transition you may want to issue the command and try just slapping the floor with the palm of your hand to get the dog moving down. Alternatively, you can place the taut leash under your left foot. As you command "Down!" apply a slight amount of pressure on the dog's shoulders. This should be sufficient to give it the idea.

As the dog progresses, you can teach it to lie down on leash from various positions, such as in front of you, from a distance, etc. You may want to incorporate a down motion with your hand in time with the "down" command. When practicing indoors, you should occasionally have the dog work off leash, but do not accept sloppy performance, as many dogs tend to be less businesslike once the lead is removed. The dog should never be allowed off leash outdoors, unless in a confined area, until it has proven itself truly trustworthy. Even then, any sudden sight or sound could distract even a well-trained terrier and cause it to bolt, so always be on your guard when the dog is off leash.

One of the most valuable commands is the "down-stay." You should train your dog to perform an extended "down-stay" *daily*. With practice, you will be able to have your dog remain in a "down-stay" for 30 minutes or more. Not only will this command reinforce your authority in the dog's mind, but it will also give you the control you need to effectively remove the dog from an undesirable activity (such as begging at your dinner table creating a scene when company comes to the door) without having to lock up the dog. This is not punishment, but rather a lesson in self-control. A properly trained dog can be placed in an extended down-stay near its owner, yet in a place where it can relax too, such as across the room or in a corner.

Begin with stays of a few minutes and then gradually increase with stays of nonuniform duration — eight minutes, then five minutes the next time, fifteen minutes the next. In this way the dog will not anticipate when it will be finished and will truly learn to obey the command. Should the dog become bored and start to break the stay, tell it "No, Stay!" and replace it. *You* must determine when the dog may rejoin you. As the dog becomes accustomed to the long "down," it will often fall asleep. This is perfectly acceptable as long as it remains where it was placed when it awakens. You should, however, wake the dog with a tap of your foot near its head when it is time to release it (try not to startle it). Do not let it sleep on after the exercise is ended; you must formally complete each exercise. Always end the long "down-stay" with the upward release motion and praise.

The "down" can also be an effective lifesaving command to immediately stop your terrier from participating in a dangerous situation. Once you are certain that the dog understands the "down" concept, the "down" can be practiced while walking, not just from the "sit."

Teaching a dog to drop down on command while in motion takes time, but is well worth the effort. For example, your well-trained terrier has been let out in the backyard; it spots a squirrel and bolts after it, ending up across the road. Upon seeing you, it abandons the chase and immediately begins to run toward you — and into oncoming traffic. *Before* the dog reaches the road, you command "Down!" and the dog immediately drops to the ground to safety. Such a case is the extreme, but it emphasizes not only the importance of the "down" command but also the fact that only an immediate response to a command is acceptable.

Both the Scottish terrier (top) and the West Highland (bottom), have been known in Scotland for hundreds of years.

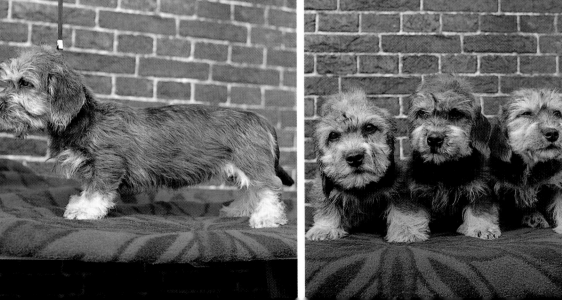

Breeding Quality Terriers

To ensure the continued quality of the terrier strains, breeding should never be haphazard. Rather, it should be a carefully planned event. The goal of dedicated breeders is to produce puppies that are of equal or better conformation than the preceding generation.

Terriers are endowed with certain traits and abilities that distinguish them from all other breeds. Random matings generally do little to retain the positive breed traits, but rather add the possibility of new faults in the offspring. The conscientious breeder's task is to select the best possible breeding partners with the goal of producing the best possible offspring.

It is my hope that all terrier fanciers who are interested enough in these wonderful breeds to be reading this book will also be dedicated enough to the future of the breeds to think carefully before breeding their dogs. The sections that follow offer guidelines for formulating a sound breeding program.

How and Why

The first step when planning a mating is to select a top-quality sire and dam. The potential sire and dam should be studied; evaluate their strengths and faults, as outlined in the breed standard. It must always be remembered that a dog's outward appearance is a result of the set of genes it received from its parents, and that a dog's outward appearance is no guarantee of the dog's ability to pass on these traits. It may have hidden traits that are not physically expressed, but that still can be passed along to offspring.

Adult Dandie Dinmont terriers (top left, bottom left) and appealing Dandie Dinmont puppies (bottom right). A poised and elegant Skye terrier (top right).

Experienced breeders determine which dogs are suitable for breeding by looking for a history of quality genes that have been passed through the family line. This is determined by reviewing pedigrees for qualities that have been consistently expressed in succeeding generations of puppies. Novice breeders wrongly assume that mating a conformation champion with a conformation champion will produce quality offspring. This may or may not happen. While sire and dam may each be of superior conformation, each may carry differing traits that do not complement the partner's; the resulting puppies may well be of lesser conformation quality than the parents.

The brood bitch is the heart of the breeding program, so care must be taken in her selection. Because of this, it may be difficult to secure a top-quality bitch from a breeder, who will be reluctant to part with a promising female puppy. Many novice breeders choose to obtain a proven quality-producing adult bitch from an established kennel (again, if the breeder will part with her), as this will eliminate some of the uncertainty of breeding a maiden dam. Such proven producers, however, are often quite expensive.

In selecting a stud terrier, a breeder has many options. The emphasis is on finding a stud that will enhance and complement the qualities of the bitch. An experienced stud that has already produced quality offspring is, of course, preferable. Whether a breeder plans to linebreed, inbreed, or outcross (see page 41), a good terrier stud should be of correct size, well-balanced, a good mover, with good coat and pigmentation, a proper bite, sound temperament, and as free of obvious faults as possible.

Beginners should seek the advice of experienced breeders whenever possible. Such a breeder can help evaluate the faults and strengths of the potential sire and dam and later evaluate the quality of the litter produced. They may also be useful in guiding the future course of your breeding program.

Breeding Quality Terriers

When considering a particular mating, begin by studying the pedigrees of the dam and sire. A pedigree was probably supplied at the time you purchased your terrier, if you bought it from an established breeder whom you informed of your possible intent to breed the dog. If not, ask the breeder to reconstruct this information, if possible. A pedigree is a very useful tool that can indicate what type of breeding system your dog stems from.

Breeding Systems

There are three types of breeding systems: linebreeding, inbreeding, and outcrossing. These systems all aim at strengthening desirable traits and eliminating faults through selective breeding, but each system pursues this goal in different ways.

Linebreeding

Linebreeding is the process of mating related dogs that are removed from each other by at least one generation (for example, grandson to grandmother, etc.). The breeding pair share a common quality ancestor (usually in the second or third generation) that is known to pass on its desirable traits to its progeny. Linebreeding enables setting or "fixing" correct type in a breeder's stock by breeding quality genes in successive generations. Linebreeding limits the flow of new genes into the breeding stock. The emphasis is on eliminating faults by establishing prepotency of desired traits. (Prepotency is the exceptional ability to transmit a trait because the animal has identical dominant genes for the trait in question.)

Inbreeding

Inbreeding is the mating of closely related dogs, with typical pairings being daughter to father, son to mother, or sister to brother. Such close matings intensify the genes present in the bloodline, as no new genes are introduced. Used very judiciously, this system can quickly fix type and bring uniformity to desired traits. Inbreeding can also bring faults to the forefront. Faults that would normally lie dormant are more likely to be expressed because of the more limited number of possible gene combinations. While producing such faulty animals is unfortunate, these faults can ultimately be eliminated, as those animals exhibiting or carrying an undesired trait are removed from the breeding program. Although controversial, inbreeding can be an effective method when used by knowledgeable, experienced breeders. It is rarely used in successive matings and is practiced in conjunction with linebreeding.

Outcrossing

Outcrossing is a system that attempts to eliminate faults by pairing parents who may complement each other. The dogs to be mated do not share common ancestors in the first five generations, but each is prepotent in traits the other lacks. This is not random selection. For example, a bitch from a line known for good hindquarters and faulty fronts would be mated with a stud dog with a strong family line of good fronts. Outcrossing is generally resorted to when linebreeding fails to correct a particular fault, and a line that is felt to be complementary is used to compensate. There are no guarantees of such a "simple" correction, however. Outcrossing adds new genes to the bloodline, rather than intensifying genes that are already present.

The mating of totally unrelated dogs is termed *outbreeding*. This is the usual pattern for the mating of neighborhood pets. If this pattern is

Breeding Quality Terriers

continued for generations, degeneration in quality and breed character is likely as the genes become a vast assortment of possibilities. First generation outbred puppies will generally be very hardy, exhibiting what is known as *hybrid vigor*. With each successive outbred generation, the faults generally become more apparent and permanently entrenched.

Starting the Breeding Program

It is best to wait until your bitch has reached maturity before breeding her, as she must be physically and mentally able to withstand the rigors of whelping and raising a litter of puppies. Do not breed her until *at least* her second heat, since at approximately 15 to 24 months of age a terrier reaches its peak of physical conditioning. A healthy terrier bitch can thereafter be bred every other season until approximately seven years of age if all previous whelpings have been uncomplicated. Some of the smaller terriers may experience difficulty in whelping, so the number of high-risk pregnancies should, of course, be limited.

A stud dog will be physically able to produce offspring when less than a year old and can continue until well into his teens. It is advisable, however, to use a stud dog that is between the ages of one and ten. At approximately eight years of age the stud's fertility begins to decline. Even though successful matings have occurred using dogs as old as 15, after the age of 12 a stud must be certified as fertile by a veterinarian in order to register any litters he has allegedly sired.

The first physical sign of the bitch's heat cycle or "season" is a marked swelling of the vulva, which becomes hard to the touch. The swelling is followed shortly by a discharge, which is watery at first and later becomes tinged with

blood—light pink at first and deepening to dark red. The bitch will be ready for mating on approximately the tenth day after the onset of her cycle. In the early days of the cycle, she is attractive to males but will not allow coitus. Ovulation generally occurs around the ninth day into the cycle, after which time she is fertile.

With most arranged stud services, the female is brought to the stud dog, as females tend to adapt more quickly to a new environment. To insure successful fertilization, the bitch is generally bred twice, with a day's interval between matings.

It is essential that the bitch and stud both be in good physical condition at the time of mating. The bitch should have been given a prebreeding examination by her veterinarian approximately one month before mating to determine her state of health and if any vaccinations or controls for internal or external parasites are needed. Be sure that both dogs are tested for canine brucellosis, a highly infectious disease that results in numerous fertility problems.

During the mating, there should always be at least two handlers present to help soothe and control the animals. The handlers should speak in subdued tones and help position the dogs if either partner is inexperienced. The stud will mount the female from the rear and grasp her around the middle with his front legs. Once the dog has penetrated the female and ejaculation has taken place, a section of his penis will swell and the dogs will be "tied" together for a period of up to 30 minutes. The handlers should remain and supervise until the tie is broken naturally. Any attempt to force uncoupling can cause serious damage—both physical and emotional—to the stud and bitch, so attention must be paid to keeping both dogs calm during this process.

Breeding Quality Terriers

Pregnancy

The normal gestation period for puppies is approximately 63 days. During the first few weeks the bitch may have a slight increase in appetite and some swelling of the breasts. The pregnancy can usually be confirmed by palpation *by a veterinarian* at 28 days after mating. *Never do this yourself!*

Throughout the pregnancy, feed the bitch the same well-balanced diet she is used to. Usually no supplementation is needed in the first four or five weeks. During the last weeks the pregnant female will need additional calories (primarily in the form of protein) to supply the requirements of the rapidly growing puppies. A food increase of 30 to 50% can be expected by whelping time; give her smaller meals three or four times daily to help avoid the discomfort that a large meal may cause her.

A pregnant bitch should continue her normal routine. It is very important for her to exercise; this will maintain muscle tone and aid in the delivery. During the last two weeks vigorous exercise, including jumping and climbing stairs, should be eliminated. As delivery approaches, the bitch will slow her activities and seek out her "nest." You should introduce her to the whelping area and allow her to adjust to it before delivery is close at hand. Otherwise, she may seek out her own, less suitable spot.

During the weeks before delivery, stock up on the following supplies and place them on a table by the whelping box: washcloths, blunt-tipped scissors, a heating pad, waxed dental floss, a scale, paper towels, a wastebasket, and a cloth-lined box to place newborns in while others are being born.

A whelping box will have to be purchased or made for the bitch to deliver the litter in and raise them for several weeks. The sides of the box should be low enough to allow the dam to come and go easily, yet high enough to keep the puppies confined while small. It should be large enough to allow the bitch to lie on her side and stretch out, but not overly large so that puppies can crawl too far from the warmth of the mother. It is advisable to build a "guard rail" several inches in width, placed several inches up the sides, to serve as a barrier that prevents the mother from inadvertently crushing the newborns against the walls. The bottom should initially be lined with renewable layers of newspaper. Be sure to place the box in a warm, dry, draft-free location away from normal family traffic.

Whelping

A bitch's temperature will drop to around 99°F (37.2°C) approximately 24 hours before delivery. Encourage her to rest. As delivery draws near, she will appear agitated and begin to pant heavily. She may vomit. The abdomen will begin contractions. A first-time mother may be very anxious at this point, so speak to her constantly in a soft, soothing tone.

You should notify your veterinarian as whelping time nears. Inexperienced breeders should also ask a more knowledgeable breeder to assist them.

Each puppy will arrive enclosed in a membrane sac, which must be removed within minutes to allow the newborn to begin breathing on its own. Should the bitch fail to tear the sac open and cut the umbilical cord, be prepared to step in quickly and perform this task. Get a briefing from your veterinarian on the entire delivery process before whelping time. The placenta (afterbirth) should be expelled within several minutes of each birth. Check that you see one placenta for each whelp, as none should be retained. Do not be surprised if the bitch eats a few of the placentas. This is quite normal and will promote milk production.

Breeding Quality Terriers

Terrier litters vary greatly in size, from approximately two or three upwards to twelve. Familiarize yourself with the normal whelping patterns of your breed, and anticipate any whelping problems that can be associated with your particular bitch and breed.

Allow the dam to lick and suckle each newborn, but remove the already born when the birth of the next whelp is in progress. At this time you can gently wipe the puppy clean, weigh it, and temporarily place it in the heated holding box until all deliveries are over.

A good brood bitch will take naturally to motherhood and exhibit a gentle touch with her puppies, as well as a tolerance for onlookers. Praise her lavishly and often for a job well done. Dams that show disinterest or aversion to their litter should be carefully monitored to prevent possible harm to the litter. Such dams are rare, and should be removed from future breeding plans.

Caring for Newborn Puppies

A warm environment—approximately 85°F (29.4°C)—is essential for the first two weeks of a newborn's life. The dam will attend to all the other basic needs of the puppies, which include not only feeding them but also stimulating them to urinate and defecate and cleaning up after them. A breeder should carefully attend to the dam's needs during the first few days and keep the whelping box very clean. Each newborn should be carefully picked up and handled on a regular basis. Check it for overall health and monitor and record its weight gain.

Puppies should receive lots of love and attention from the earliest days; this will begin a human-dog bond. Newborns can be gently stroked, caressed, and softly spoken to from

This whelping box has plenty of space for the mother and puppies and is high enough to keep the newborns in without restricting the mother's freedom.

A puppy must always be properly supported when being lifted. Place one hand against the rib cage and the other under the puppy's rear end.

birth. Such stimulation has been shown to heighten their awareness and ability to interact with humans. The puppies' eyes and ears will begin to open at about 10 days, and stimulations such as soft music and colorful visual backgrounds encourage prompt development of the senses.

The weaning process can begin at approximately three weeks of age. This begins the transition to adulthood; the puppy will be required to master canine and human socialization in just a few week's time—as well as learn to run and frolic like a thrill-seeking puppy. Breeders should take time to handle each puppy as much as possible, giving each a daily grooming with a soft brush. This grooming will require the wriggling puppy to submit to its human master and is the first introduction to the human "alpha" figure.

Puppies can begin weaning at approximately three weeks of age; begin with a thin gruel to accustom them to lapping up solid foods.

Feeding Your Terrier

The selection of your dog's daily food is a decision that should not be taken lightly. It will have a direct impact on the dog's overall health and longevity. The primary concern is to select food that is nutritionally complete and balanced.

While most owners of a limited number of animals will make their pet food selection from the brands available in their local supermarket, this is not the only option. The foods used by the larger commercial kennels are also available in small quantities from many pet shops and suppliers. Most of the popular brands are the product of much research into canine nutrition. One must still do a bit of comparative shopping before deciding on a brand, as the most popular brand may not be the best food for your dog.

Types of Food

The main types of dog food are dry, semimoist, canned, and supplementary. No one type alone is completely satisfactory; most owners find a blend of several to be the best solution.

Dry Food

This is the most commonly used type of dog food, and also the type most likely to vary in quality. Dry foods are generally composed of 8 to 10% water; the remaining ingredients are cereals, soy, meat by-products, and small amounts of fats, vitamins, and minerals. Ounce for ounce this is the least expensive type of dog food, and in the long run it may be the most healthful.

The most popular "name" brands are nutritionally complete products; look for the list of nutritional values on the package. There may be great variation, however, in the amount of dry food that must be consumed to fulfill the basic dietary requirements. With some dry products an excessive amount must be eaten to fulfill your dog's needs. This can be determined by reading the suggested feeding amounts per weight of dog as listed on the package. If large amounts must be ingested, there will be an inevitable increase in waste materials to be excreted. Also content may vary from batch to batch in many dry food products, as fluctuations in the availability of the base crop (soy, corn, barley, etc.) produce a slightly different blending at various times during the year.

The "professional" meat-and-meal based dry foods commonly used by commercial breeders and sold in pet supply houses offer a stable mixture from batch to batch. These dry food brands are nutritionally complete, easily digested, and formulated with enough fiber to help produce a firm stool. The suggested feeding amounts are sufficient to fulfill all nutritional requirements without forcing the dog to overeat. Although these products may cost a little more per pound, in the long run they may be less expensive, as the dog does not need to eat as much of it.

One drawback of dry food products is that they tend to be low in fat. This is easily handled by adding approximately half a container of canned food to the dry food as a supplement.

Semimoist Food

The semimoist foods are highly processed; they are usually packaged in pouches or shaped as "hamburgers." They generally contain 25% water and are composed primarily of soy meal, meat by-products, and cereal. Although these products have been improved significantly in recent years, this type of food is very expensive on a cost-per-ounce basis and still contains a considerable amount of additives and preservatives. While the levels of sugar and salt have been decreased, semimoist products are still very high in calories. While the high level of processing creates a product with a color and an odor that is pleasing to the *human* eye (dogs couldn't care less), it can also produce an allergic reaction in some dogs. This often takes the form of hyperactivity or skin biting or scratching in sensitive dogs.

It is recommended that semimoist foods be used only in conjunction with a high-quality dry food, with the semimoist comprising no more than one quarter of the daily intake. Semimoist products can also be of use when a dog needs to put on some weight, as it is a very appealing food for most dogs.

Canned Food

Canned dog food is very popular, but based on its content it is very expensive. Most canned dog foods contain approximately 75% water, and the remaining 25% is generally meat by-products, soy fillers, vitamins, minerals, artificial coloring, and preservatives. The high water level and additives can have a diuretic effect on many dogs, and this can result in housebreaking problems.

Some canned foods are more nutritious than others, with the ones designed for the various stages of life most recommended. Even these should not comprise the entire diet, but should form no more than one quarter of the daily intake. Canned food should be combined with a high-quality dry food for best results. Most dogs are very fond of canned food, so this is also recommended for dogs needing to gain some weight.

Supplements

Millions of dollars have been spent by leading pet food companies to create nutritionally complete products. Adding things to a basic diet can upset the nutritional balance. Raising a dog strictly on home-prepared meals is unadvisable, unless undertaken with supervision from a nutritionist.

Unlike humans, dogs are not easily bored by a satisfactory diet and can eat the same food every day. However, giving your dog an occasional treat or nutritious snack will do no harm. Since commercially prepared diets can be lacking in roughage, this aspect of the diet can be improved by giving your dog a daily raw carrot, apple, or crunchy biscuit.

Table scraps can be too much of a good thing. While your dog will undoubtedly love fatty meat scraps, the result may be a case of loose bowels. Small snacks of fruits, vegetables, and cereals will not upset the intestinal tract and may, in fact, help promote proper digestion. The trick is to get the dog trained to enjoy these snacks while still a puppy, as a dog raised on snacks of steak will be less than enthusiastic about a change to such healthful snacks.

Crunchy foods, such as carrots or a sturdy veal bone, can also serve to keep the teeth clean by scraping away tartar along the tooth surface. Be very selective with bones, however, as these can be not only constipating but also potentially deadly; an ingested splinter of bone can penetrate internal organs and do extensive damage. Sturdy nylon or rawhide bones are safest; they can be purchased in pet shops, supermarkets, and specialty shops.

Aside from nursing mothers, most dogs will be able to fulfill all their dietary needs through commercially prepared dog food and will seldom need vitamin supplements. Problems caused by excessive vitamin supplementation are more common than ones from vitamin deficiencies from commercially prepared foods. It is especially important not to oversupplement the diet of growing puppies, as there can be serious side effects. A well-balanced diet, supported by adequate exercise, should be all your dog needs to keep in good trim and good health.

Feeding Your Terrier

The Feeding Process

Not only is *what* you feed your dog of utmost importance, you must also form a pattern for *where, when,* and *how* you feed your dog. These may seem like lesser concerns, but they help establish a healthy routine.

Where should you feed your dog? Contrary to the notion that Rocco enjoys eating in the middle of the kitchen floor while the family is scurrying around (he's part of the "family" that way), it should be remembered that dogs have pack instincts, not human traits. They should be allowed adequate time and space to eat their meal in an out-of-the-way place. In the bustle of the kitchen at a busy time of day the dog may be anxious that its food is in danger of being taken away and may develop bad habits in response. One common reaction is to quickly devour the food. Such a habit can lead to digestive problems or a pattern whereby the dog eats too quickly, vomits back the food, and eats it once again. Eating in a high-traffic area also can make the dog overprotective of its food, which certainly is to be avoided. A dog must be trained from an early age to allow its master to pick up and remove the food, if necessary, without the dog's growling or protesting.

When to feed your dog depends mostly on the age of the dog and the daily routine of master and dog. Young puppies will require four or five small meals a day. This can be reduced to three daily meals at approximately four to six months, with a further reduction to two daily meals at approximately nine months of age. The usual adult dog feeding schedule is either one large meal a day, generally in the late afternoon or at night, or two smaller meals daily.

How you feed your dog refers not only to the process but to quantity. There can be no set scale for how much food one dog will need daily. The amount listed on the package label should be taken only as a guide, for each dog has a different metabolism and lifestyle. An active, hard-working terrier will require more calories per day than an older, slow-moving one. Growing puppies and pregnant or lactating bitches will need a diet high in protein and calories.

To promote healthy eating patterns, keep the feeding process simple. Give the dog some privacy and ample time to eat its meal—generally 15 to 20 minutes. After this time, pick up and discard any leftover food. At the next meal reduce the amount slightly if the dog has been leaving food uneaten; you need to determine the approximate amount needed for the dog to be satisfied and clear its bowl. If the bowl is quickly cleared, you may need to increase the amount slightly. If the dog is still actively eating when you come to retrieve the bowl, give it another five minutes or so.

If the dog refuses its food, pick it up and discard it. Do not offer a replacement until the next scheduled meal. Catering to a picky eater will only enhance the problem. If the refusal continues for more than a few meals and the dog seems hungry and healthy, you may want to change the diet *one time* to verify if the dog really does have an aversion to the food you have been offering. As previously mentioned, some brands do modify the contents of their product from batch to batch, so the food may really be distasteful to your dog. However, a sudden distaste for eating is generally an indication of either a health or a behavioral problem. The food is probably fine. If the problem persists, have the dog examined by a veterinarian. If given a clean bill of health, remember that dogs will test the leadership of their owners from time to time. Once it learns that you will not give in, it will.

The point to remember is to keep the process simple: place the dog in its secluded eating spot, give it the food, leave it alone, and clean up when finished. Never whine or nag the dog to eat, as it will sense your insecurity and exploit it. Terriers can be quite manipulative if given an opening by a well-meaning owner.

A few additional feeding rules are:

• Have an ample supply of clean, fresh water available at all times. This is especially important in hot weather.

• Clean all food and water bowls daily in hot, soapy water and rinse well to inhibit the growth of bacteria.

• Do not make sudden changes in the diet. To avoid digestive upset, introduce new foods slowly, in modest amounts.

• Always bring a supply of the dog's usual food when traveling or when the dog must be kenneled.

• Do not leave the water bowl available all night if the dog is having problems with housebreaking. Eliminating the source of the liquid may help eliminate the problem.

• Serve the food at room temperature, not cold from the refrigerator.

Several types of food and water dishes are available. All are sturdy; some include food and water dishes in the same stand.

Teething and Chewing

While terriers are not noted as compulsive chewers, *all dogs will chew*. It is a natural process, and owners should be aware of it. A puppy will chew to help cut its first teeth, to exercise and strengthen its jaw, and to rid itself of the first teeth. As you can see, a puppy may do a lot of chewing between four and nine months of age. But don't be fooled into thinking it will all end in a few months. The need to chew will remain as the dog matures.

A dog will need to rid itself of accumulated tartar on the teeth, and the best method for this is through chewing hard substances. Since there is little of this in the basic diet, other objects must be found. Some dogs also use chewing as a method to release tension, often causing extensive and expensive damage to household goods.

Since there is no simple method to stop chewing, the best course is prevention. Be prepared and on your guard. Give the dog an ample supply of suitable chew objects and let the dog know what *may* and *may not* be chewed. Do not give the dog an old slipper to chew and then expect it to leave your best oxfords alone.

Rawhide bones are favorites with most dogs, but these can prove to be quite expensive as many dogs can devour them in short order. Nylon bones are long-lasting, safe alternatives, but many dogs find them unappealing. Hard veal bones, such as from the knuckle, should be given sparingly, as they can be constipating as well as too abrasive to the tooth enamel if the dog is a prodigious chewer. Many dogs enjoy chewing on hard rubber balls that are large enough to mouth but not swallow.

During the initial teething stages, confine the dog when it cannot be supervised and give it a suitable chew toy. A crate is best for this (more on crates on page 26). Do not be fooled into thinking

thinking that the chewing stage is over when the first teeth are shed—an *intense* need to chew will occur when the back molars come in. Many people are unprepared for this renewed bout with chewing and have suffered great losses at this time.

When the dog is allowed to roam about the home, monitor it and, for your own protection, remove all chewable temptations. A dog must be taught what is allowable and what is not, and unfortunately this is a trial-and-error process. When you catch the dog with a forbidden object in its mouth, immediately remove it from the dog's clutches, shake it in front of the dog's head and tap it as you say "No!" in a stern voice. If the misdeed is repeated, add a shake of the dog's neck to your correction and banish the dog with a lengthy "down-stay" (see page 36) or a trip to its crate.

Chewing can be destructive not only to your household goods, it can also be fatal for the dog. Electric cords are appealing to the inquisitive puppy and can be deadly if plugged in. Some plants are poisonous if ingested, and many dogs are attracted to them by their smell or appearance. If you have poisonous plants, such as poinsettia, be sure they are inaccessible to the dog.

Health Care

On the whole, terriers are a rugged group not prone to many out-of-the-ordinary illnesses. This hardiness should not be taken for granted; it hinges on good everyday care, the availability of a nutritious diet, and ample exercise. In addition, every dog needs routine veterinary checkups and required vaccinations throughout its life. I cannot recommend too strongly that you consult a veterinarian shortly after you notice symptoms of illness in your terrier. Delaying treatment can be a costly mistake. Many illnesses that are easily handled in the early stages can become life-threatening if treatment is delayed.

This Kerry blue terrier is being groomed with a slicker brush.

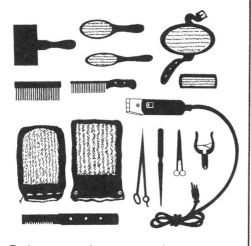

Terrier coats come in many types and textures. Groomers require an array of grooming tools to deal with each breed's particular requirements. Pictured are various types of brushes, combs, hound gloves, clippers, and trimming aids.

Conscientious owners monitor the overall health of their pets by regularly inspecting exposed areas (eyes, ears, feet, skin, and teeth) for signs of discharge, abrasions, or sensitivity. This should become a regular routine during the grooming process. Begin by running your hands over the dog's entire body and feeling for anything unusual, such as cysts, sores, and areas that are swollen or cause the dog pain when touched. For breeds with tough double coats, be sure to get down to the skin and look and feel for signs of irritation. Next, you should turn to the head and begin a more thorough examination.

Routine Care

Problems that are caught promptly are usually much easier to deal with, so be on the lookout for the early stages of disorders. The eyes, ears, and feet are particularly vulnerable in terriers, as these body parts often get right in on the digging and hunting actions that delight terriers.

Ears
The ears should be routinely inspected for foreign objects (dirt, burrs, bugs) and scratches. Symptoms of ear problems are a constant shaking of the head, rubbing the ears (with the paws or on the ground), excessive earwax, redness, swelling, or a foul odor from the ear canal. These symptoms will require a veterinarian's attention.

A bristle brush will help keep this Boston terrier's coat tidy.

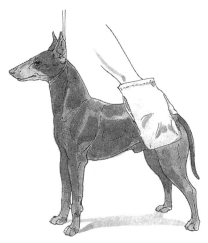

This Manchester terrier is being groomed with a hound glove.

You can see into the dog's ear by using a small flashlight, but *never* probe inside the ear canal; this can be extremely painful for the dog and can greatly damage this very sensitive organ. To reduce the normal buildup of wax and dirt in the ear, routinely swab the easily reached areas with a cotton ball dampened with warm water. If cleanliness is a continual problem, ointments made specially for cleaning the *outer* ear can be bought from pet shops, grooming parlors, or your veterinarian. Avoid oily compounds; their sticky residue may, in fact, *attract and retain* dirt. If you suspect that the ear is heavily laden with wax, let your veterinarian do a more thorough cleaning. If the problem is chronic, ask for instructions to perform this procedure at home.

The most common ear irritations are simple abrasions, which will require a salve to reduce the sting and promote healing. Your veterinarian can tell you what salve to apply.

If your terrier shows increased sensitivity when you touch its ears, an infection may be present.

Otitis, an inflammation of the inner or outer ear, can be treated locally. Possible causes of the inflammation are parasites (such as mites) or bacteria. For appropriate treatment, accurate diagnosis is required, so seek veterinary assistance at first sign of a problem. Do not use over-the-

A pin brush will help remove snarls in this soft-coated wheaten's coat.

Health Care

Should the dog's coat become matted, carefully separate the hairs by hand before attempting to comb the coat through.

When bathing, begin at the head and work down the coat. Pay particular attention to keeping the water from entering the dog's ears.

An ungroomed Yorkshire terrier.

A well-groomed Yorkshire terrier.

counter ointments unless so instructed by your veterinarian. Deafness can be the tragic result of incorrectly treated or untreated ear infections.

Eyes

It is not uncommon for some terriers to produce a slight discharge around the eyes that can be easily cleared away with a damp, lint-free cloth. If this discharge becomes excessive, or if your dog blinks constantly and one or both eyes are red, consult your veterinarian. Small external eye lesions may be caused by low vegetation, and minor internal irritations may result when tiny particles are caught under the eyelids. These occurrences will normally be slightly painful for the dog and any scratches should quickly heal without treatment. Minor irritations can quickly become serious, however, so special attention should be paid to a constant discharge or pawing of the eye area.

Terriers' eyes are quite susceptible to injury and should be routinely inspected.

Feet

Working terriers (and those pets that *feel* like working terriers) do a great deal of digging, which makes their paws susceptible to various minor injuries. The pads of your terrier's feet should be inspected regularly, especially if the dog limps or favors a leg. Burrs, splinters, or stones can become caught in and between the pads of the foot, and scratches are quite common. For minor problems, a cleaning with warm soapy water may be sufficient. If necessary, use sterilized tweezers to remove foreign objects, and apply a mild antiseptic.

If your dog suddenly begins to limp and favor or lick one foot, an insect bite could be the cause. If you suspect this, apply an ice compress to reduce or prevent swelling and ease the pain. Unless there is an allergic reaction (see Stinging Insects, page 60), this condition should pass quickly.

If there is no evidence of a cut or sting, and the dog indicates pain in the foot, there may be an injury to the bones or muscles of the area or there may be an object deeply embedded in the footpad. Both these conditions require diagnosis by a veterinarian.

If you live in a snowy climate, you need to protect your dog's feet from snow-melting chemicals on sidewalks, as these are caustic to a dog's footpads and skin. When you return home after a walk, rinse your terrier's feet with warm, soapy water. Pay special attention to drying between the toes. Salts and sand caught in these spaces by the short, matted hairs will lead to painful irritations. A little talcum powder will help, also. When thoroughly dry, apply a thin layer of petroleum jelly to soothe any irritation. Remember, too, that if bothered by these chemicals, the dog might lick its feet to relieve discomfort. Ingesting such poisonous materials is, of course, hazardous to your pet's health.

Health Care

Trimming Nails

Terriers are by nature an energetic, active group, but many of today's terriers do not get extensive outside exercise and exposure to rough ground required to keep the nails naturally trimmed. Most house pets need to have their nails regularly trimmed, as overgrown nails can interfere with normal placement of the foot and affect a dog's gait.

Nail trimming requires the use of a specially designed clipper, available from pet stores, grooming parlors, and veterinarians. If you are inexperienced, have your veterinarian teach you the simple nail-trimming procedure, so you can easily do it at home. Be sure to cut only the outer shell of the nail; cutting too close to the quick can cause bleeding. Once the nail is shortened to the proper length, smooth the surface with a few brushes of an emery board. If you cut too close to the quick and the nail bleeds, apply pressure to the area by holding a cotton swab over the nail. Once the bleeding stops, dab the nail with a mild antiseptic, such as peroxide.

Tooth Care

Tartar is a lifelong problem for dogs, just as for humans—only a dog can't brush its own teeth or make semiannual trips to a dental hygienist. A diet that includes foods naturally abrasive to the teeth (such as carrots) is highly recommended. Chewing a safe, hard bone will help keep teeth clean by removing most buildup.

It is advisable to accustom your terrier from puppyhood to having its teeth gently cleaned with a soft brush or moistened gauze pad. If you notice a yellowing of the tooth exterior, which is common as the dog ages, further treatment may be needed. The teeth can be brushed once or twice a week with a mild paste of baking soda and hydrogen peroxide to remove stains and plaque. The paste can be applied with a child's toothbrush. This procedure may be frightening and irritating to your terrier, so talk to it in a re-assuring tone but be firm and do not allow the dog to balk at the cleaning.

If discoloring remains despite weekly brushings, the teeth may need to be scaled by your veterinarian. Since a dog will need its teeth throughout its life, all measures should be taken to insure and protect its health. If the buildup is chronic, your veterinarian may wish to teach you to perform this scaling procedure at home as part of the dog's regular grooming.

A heavy accumulation of tartar will require removal by a veterinarian.

Many tooth problems are not revealed by the outward condition or color of the teeth. A sudden change in the dog's breath that lasts for more than a few days may indicate a problem with the teeth (or could be a symptom of an internal condition). Decayed teeth may also make it painful for the dog to eat. If you suspect a tooth problem, inspect the teeth and gums for any obvious sign of infection, swelling, bleeding, or sensitivity to the touch. An abscessed tooth sometimes produces a swelling on the cheek area. Your veterinarian should be informed as soon as you notice any of these conditions.

Terriers are intelligent animals that respond eagerly to a challenge. Airedales are shown jumping barriers and retrieving.

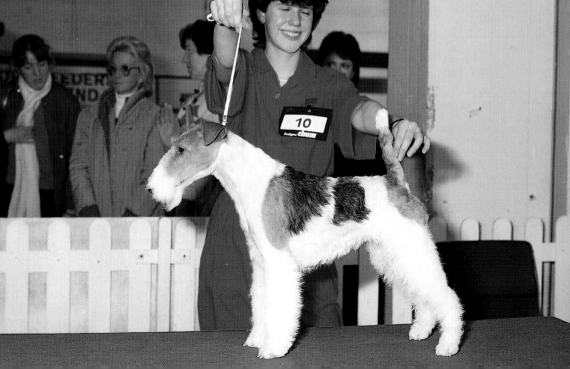

Health Care

Simple Health Care Procedures

There are a number of simple procedures that every dog owner should master. These include taking a dog's temperature and pulse, and giving it medication.

Taking the Dog's Temperature

A dog's normal temperature is slightly higher than a human's—100° to 101.5°F (37.7°–38°C). Begin by lubricating the end of a heavy-duty rectal thermometer with a little petroleum jelly. It is best to have an assistant nearby to help restrain the dog during the insertion and to prevent the dog from injuring itself by sitting down or otherwise breaking the thermometer. It is best to have the dog stand, but it can also lie on its side. One person should get a secure grasp on the dog while the other lifts the tail and inserts the thermometer. The thermometer should remain for two to three minutes for an accurate reading.

When taking a dog's temperature, be sure the dog is properly restrained to avoid any possible injury.

With all their liveliness, terriers take readily to the discipline of the dog show. A Lakeland terrier (top) and a Wire fox terrier (bottom) vying for honors.

Giving the Dog Medication

Another procedure most dog owners have to face is giving their dog medication. There are several methods, depending on the type and amount of medicine required. Giving a dog a pill or capsule may seem simple enough, but more is required than just popping the pill into Rocco's mouth. Most dogs quickly master the technique for *not* swallowing pills, and defiantly spit them right out. The easiest (and sneakiest) method is to disguise the pill in something tasty, such as a small chunk of hamburger meat or a piece of cheese that is quickly swallowed in one gulp. If the dog swallows it happily, consider yourself lucky. If not, you will have to gently pry the dog's mouth open by applying pressure at the back of its jaws, tilt the head up *slightly*, and insert the pill as far back on the tongue as possible. Close the jaws and look for a swallow. Gently stroking the throat may help the cause. *Never lift the dog's head straight up; this can lead to having the pill inhaled into the windpipe rather than being swallowed.*

When administering liquid medicine, place it in a medicine spoon or syringe and pour it into the *back of the mouth* by lifting up the side of the dog's lower lip by the back molars and holding the head *slightly* upward. This allows the medicine to slide down the throat. Keep a grasp around the dog's muzzle until you are sure it has swallowed, or the dog may easily spit the medicine out. Again, never hold the head in an exaggerated upward position, as this invites choking.

Liquid and powdered medicines may also be mixed into the dog's food; check this with your veterinarian first, however. But many dogs spot the additives right away and won't touch the food. If this is the case, the powdered medications can usually be liquefied by adding a little water, and you can proceed as described above.

Health Care

Taking The Dog's Pulse

A potentially lifesaving procedure you can easily perform is to monitor the dog's heartbeat. A dog's normal heartbeat is 70 to 90 beats per minute, but may vary with such factors as age, temperature, exertion, stress, and illness. A pulse can be found in the front paw, but the one located on the inside of the thigh is the easiest to read. Press softly against the pulse and monitor the pattern and rate of the beats. This procedure should be performed if you ever notice signs of extreme fatigue, fainting, or hyperactivity in your dog. Any abnormal patterns in the heartbeat require immediate attention by a veterinarian.

A muzzle can be applied to prevent a nervous dog from snapping when undergoing veterinary procedures.

Examinations and Vaccinations

Regardless of the condition of your dog, it should get an annual physical examination by your veterinarian, who will evaluate the dog's general condition, test for internal parasites, and determine if the dog needs any inoculations. By keeping current with the required vaccinations you can protect your dog from many of the infectious diseases that have proven to be killers. Most puppies receive their first immunizations while still with their breeder. These include, at around five to eight weeks of life, initial vaccinations for distemper, hepatitis, parvovirus, leptospirosis, and parainfluenza. A follow-up series will be required for most vaccines, on a schedule devised by your veterinarian. A rabies vaccination will also be needed, as well as boosters as the dog matures to help insure continued immunity.

Be sure to get from the breeder the records of your dog's earliest shots and pass this information along to your veterinarian. This is vital information for your dog's health record. At the initial checkup and then annually the dog may be tested for the presence of worms, and treated if necessary. Ask the breeder if the dog has already been tested and treated for worms. If it has, find out what type of worm the dog was infected with, what medication was used to treat it, and how the dog reacted to the medication. Worms are very common in puppies, and this background information can be very helpful in accurately assessing the dog's health.

Worms

As mentioned, worms are very common in dogs, especially puppies. Worms should never be ignored, however; left unchecked, worms can be very debilitating and sometimes life-threatening. Diagnosing the type of worm present in a dog and devising the remedy should be left strictly to the veterinarian. Routine wormings of a dog using over-the-counter preparations are unnecessary and can be extremely dangerous.

Symptoms of worm infestation include weight loss, weakness, a bloated stomach, diarrhea, poor coat sheen, loss of appetite, or, alternatively, a voracious appetite. The dog may exhibit signs of distress such as dragging its anus across the ground, or licking and biting around the tail area. Some infected dogs will give little outward sign of the problem until heavily infested, which points out the importance of having the dog checked at least annually.

Detecting the presence of most worms is done by microscopic examination of stool or blood samples. The most common types of worm are the roundworm, tapeworm, hookworm, and heartworm. Each requires a specific medicine to effect a cure. In the case of heartworm, a disease primarily spread by mosquitoes, once the dog has been shown by blood test to be free of the parasite, a *preventive* medication can be administered daily throughout mosquito season to keep the dog free from infestation.

The most important point to remember about worming is that a proper diagnosis by an expert and the administration of the proper medication in the proper dosage are the keys to eliminating the problem. Indiscriminately worming a dog can be deadly; all too frequently well-intentioned owners overdose their pets.

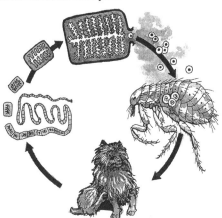

The life cycle of the dog tapeworm: Tapeworm eggs are ingested by fleas and hatch in the fleas' intestines. Should a dog ingest an infected flea, the tapeworms mature in the dog's intestines. The mature tapeworms in turn lay eggs that are passed in the dog's stool. Tapeworm eggs can also be ingested by eating uncooked meat or fish.

Fleas and Ticks

Fleas and ticks are a nasty fact of life. They infest a host, bite its skin, suck its blood, itch unbearably, and often infect the dog with tapeworm. Terriers are earth dogs, and external parasites will be found almost everywhere on earth that these dogs care to go. The severity of the problem may depend on the local climate and the type of coat the dog has. Breeds with wiry double coats may suffer from flea infestation and skin irritations without outward signs of the problems, so owners must be diligent to routinely inspect the dog's skin, especially if the dog is scratching or biting itself.

Fleas

Ridding a dog of fleas takes diligence. Powders and sprays designed especially for this purpose can be purchased at any pet store or grooming parlor. The coat must be thoroughly doused with the repellent in order for it to work; the active ingredient must reach the skin. Be extremely careful when applying the material, as it can do great damage to the dog's mucous membranes. Cover the dog's eyes, ears, nose, and mouth and slowly work the powder into the coat, working against the grain.

For heavy infestations, a bath with a flea dip will be needed. Many grooming parlors will do this as a service, or you can do it at home. Always use products designed just for this purpose, and read all directions before beginning.

Once the dog has been cleared of fleas, you will have to make sure that the house, especially the dog's bedding, is also free of parasites. If the fleas have found their way into the household carpeting, a heavy-duty insect bomb (available at most hardware stores and pet shops) will be needed to destroy all the breeding colonies.

These measures will temporarily take care of the problem, but the battle against fleas will usually go on as long as the weather sustains them.

A flea collar will help protect the dog from reinfection. Be sure to take the collar off if it gets wet, as it can become irritating to the skin.

Ticks

Ticks, another common problem for terriers, should not be taken lightly; they are disease carriers and can be painful for the afflicted dog. Once on their host, ticks gnaw through the skin and implant themselves so that they can suck and live off the dog's blood.

Removing a tick must be done carefully. If a tick is simply ripped from the skin, the head can tear away from the body and remain embedded in the skin. This often results in an infection or abscess. The proper way to remove a tick is to grasp it firmly, as close to the skin as possible, using a tweezer or your thumb and forefinger, and apply firm but gentle upward pressure. Do not twist. An alternative method is to apply a tick dip, which can be purchased from most veterinarians or pet shops. This will, in effect, suffocate the tick and make it release its hold on the dog's skin. *Never try to burn off a tick with a match or a cigarette.* The dangers of this should be evident. Once a tick has been removed, a small lump or swollen area may remain for several days.

There are numerous external parasites that can attack a dog. An owner's responsibility is to keep an eye on the dog's general health, paying close attention to the outward appearance of the coat, especially during the warm summer months. Infestations by lice or mites are not uncommon and can result in uncontrollable itching and scratching in afflicted dogs. This can lead to great damage to the dog's coat and skin that may take a long time to heal, so it is important to catch skin problems in the early stages. If you notice any clusters of eggs, a rash of bumps, or pustules on the skin, consult your veterinarian for proper diagnosis and treatment.

Stinging Insects

Bee and insect bites are generally difficult to detect. If you happen to witness your dog being bitten, check the site and see if the stinger is still embedded. If it is, carefully remove it by scraping your fingernail across the base of the bite using a scooping motion. This will limit the spread of the venom. If possible, apply ice or a cold compress to the area to reduce swelling and slow the flow of the toxin to other areas.

While a bug bite will usually be little more than a momentary discomfort for the dog, it can also be life-threatening. Occasionally, a dog will have an allergic reaction to a bite. Reactions will vary from dog to dog, depending on level of sensitivity. A case of hives or localized swelling will generally subside within hours, with no lasting effect. A more severe reaction, such as marked swelling or difficulty in breathing, requires immediate veterinary attention. For most cases, administering some over-the-counter antihistamine (as advised by your veterinarian) or a corticosteroid will relieve symptoms. If your dog exhibits a marked tendency toward allergy to stinging insects, consult your veterinarian and devise a strategy for future emergencies, with antidotes available at all times.

A tick, before feeding (left) and after feeding (right).

Health Care

Emergency Procedures

In emergencies speed is most important. If your dog sustains a serious injury, you must act quickly to stabilize the dog's condition until you can transport the animal to a veterinarian. Your first act must be to calm and restrain the dog. You cannot let the dog move about; this may lead to further damage. There may be internal problems not visible to the eye. You must also protect yourself from being bitten. The dog is terrified and may lash out at anyone that comes near it, so be sure to approach the animal carefully. Speak to it in low, soothing tones. A stocking, a tie, or a thin piece of cloth will serve as an emergency muzzle. Fold the material in half, placing the center fold on the top of the muzzle. Cross the two bands of material under the bottom of the jaw and bring them around to the back of the head. Tie a secure knot, but be sure it is not too restrictive. You are now ready to assess the dog's physical condition.

Wounds and Fractures

Never move an injured animal unless absolutely necessary, such as to remove it from a site where it may incur further damage. Inspect the skin and locate the source of any bleeding. If possible, gently wash the area with soap and warm water. If blood continues to flow, apply a clean cloth or gauze pad, secure it if possible, and hold the compress in place until the bleeding stops. Unless the cut is very small, it will need professional attention. A veterinarian will be better able to apply a bandage that will stay in place.

If it appears that a bone has been broken, immobilize the dog to the best of your ability. If allowed to move about, the dog may do damage to the muscles, cartilage, and nerves surrounding the break. Try to keep the dog calm and get it to emergency treatment as quickly as possible. If necessary, you can use a blanket as a makeshift stretcher for transporting the dog short distances.

If the dog lapses into unconsciousness, check that its breathing passages are open. Get the dog onto its side. Gently pry open its mouth and pull the tongue forward to allow air to flow into the lungs.

In all these situations, shock can quickly set in. Cover the dog with a blanket for added warmth and monitor its heart rate. This information may be useful for the attending veterinarian.

Poisonings

Most accidental poisonings occur without the owner ever knowing that the dog has ingested a poisonous substance. This often has serious consequences, since *immediate* action is generally required for the dog to have a good chance of survival. Symptoms of poisoning include diarrhea, vomiting, lethargy, spasms, shaking, dizziness, and a color change or bleeding of the mucous membranes.

If you know the cause of the poisoning and are lucky enough to have access to the packaging, look for information on the proper antidote. Your local poison control center may also be of help. Knowing how much poison was swallowed, and when, will greatly help your veterinarian to chart the treatment. Various procedures may be required, depending on the type of poison: sometimes the stomach can be pumped, sometimes specific antidotes can neutralize the poison in the stomach. Without adequate information on what happened, the veterinarian has little to go on and the outcome can be grave.

Terriers are inquisitive animals; this character trait can lead to trouble. Household items are the most common sources of poisoning, not only for children but also for house pets. Many house and garden plants are poisonous if chewed or eaten. Included among these are philodendron, poinsettia, and daffodil bulbs. Keep locked all cleaning agents, pesticides, and painting supplies. Antifreeze is particularly dangerous, as it is highly poisonous but has a pleasant odor and taste that attract the dog.

Health Care

Common Illnesses

Most dogs contract a few minor illnesses in the course of their lives; these disorders will hopefully be no more serious than passing upsets in humans. Dogs, however, often cannot communicate their discomforts to their owners, so it is up to you to monitor your terrier's condition and decide whether veterinary attention is required.

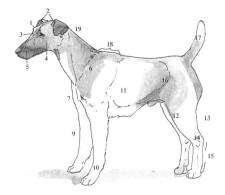

The structure of a smooth fox terrier. Knowledge of your pet's external and internal anatomy will help you communicate with your veterinarian.

1. skull	7. chest	13. hindquarters
2. ears	8. brisket	14. hock
3. stop	9. forequarters	15. rear pastern
4. cheek	10. front pastern	16. loin
5. muzzle	11. ribcage	17. tail
6. shoulder	12. stifle	18. withers
		19. neckline

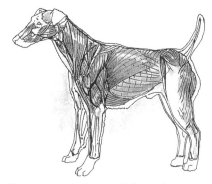

The musculature of a smooth fox terrier.

Vomiting

Various illnesses that involve the digestive tract will lead to vomiting. Most incidents are quick to pass and are often related to something the dog has eaten. Severe, continued vomiting is very serious, however, and can lead to dehydration.

If the vomiting is limited to a few episodes, the first step is to withhold all food for 12 to 24 hours. You can administer some Pepto-Bismol® to help settle the dog's stomach and allow a few sips of water. If there is no sign of fever and the vomiting lets up, you can give the dog several small, bland meals during the next 24 hours. If the vomiting does not recur, the normal diet can be resumed the following day. If vomiting continues or intensifies, or if you notice any blood or worms in the vomit, get the dog to a veterinarian at first opportunity.

While terriers on the whole are not given to unusual eating patterns, some dogs have a tendency to gulp their food. This, in turn, may result in a sudden regurgitation of the meal due to the presence of too much air in the stomach. If your terrier is prone to this behavior, the best solution is to serve several small meals each day rather than one or two large ones, thereby limiting the amount of food in the stomach at any one time and the need to vomit.

Diarrhea

Like vomiting, a mild case of diarrhea may have many causes, most of which are not serious or life-threatening. As with vomiting, the first step is to withhold food for the next 12 to 24 hours to allow the system to rid itself of any offending material in the intestinal tract. A small amount of water is permissible, however, as is a dose of Kaopectate® to help soothe the intestines. If symptoms do not worsen during the next 24 hours, the dog can be allowed several small, bland meals containing a binding agent such as rice or oatmeal.

If you ever notice a bloody discharge, or if the diarrhea does not stop, veterinary assistance is needed. Diarrhea combined with vomiting and/or a high fever can be symptoms of a serious problem, so do not delay in getting help from a trained professional.

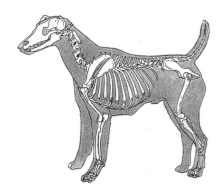

The skeleton of a smooth fox terrier.

Constipation

Constipation most often occurs when the dog undergoes a sudden dietary change. However, a dog that is confined for too long may also bring on this problem by restraining its natural urges to eliminate until given access to the proper site. In such cases, the problem is usually temporary and can generally be relieved by administering a mild laxative, such as milk of magnesia. Ask your veterinarian for the proper dosage, based on your dog's weight. If your terrier tends to be constipated, add a little extra roughage to the dog's normal diet to aid proper elimination. If the condition lingers, your veterinarian may suggest remedial use of a glycerine suppository or a warm water enema.

Constipation can be a serious problem if not relieved, and can be brought on by a variety of causes. Should you ever see the dog actively straining, crying out with pain, and not passing any excrement, seek professional care at once. The dog might have swallowed an object that is now lodged in the intestinal tract, causing a life-threatening situation. Alternatively, there could be a tumor or other growth in the intestines. Such situations are emergencies that require specialized veterinary care.

Anal Gland Disorders

At the base of the dog's anus are two glands that secrete a strong-smelling substance used by the dog as a scent marker. These glands, sometimes referred to as the "stink glands," are normally emptied during defecation. If, however, the glands are not completely cleared by the normal elimination process, they can become impacted, and require manual emptying. The symptoms of impacted anal glands include a constant licking of the area and/or dragging the anus across the ground or floor. (This is also symptomatic of worm infestation, however.) If the anal glands appear full, they can be manually expressed by

Health Care

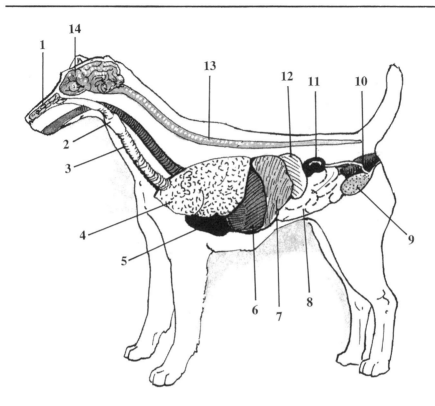

Internal organs (a smooth fox terrier is used for this demonstration).

1. sinus cavity
2. thyroid cartilage
3. trachea
4. lungs
5. heart
6. liver
7. stomach
8. small intestine
9. bladder
10. rectum
11. kidneys
12. spleen
13. spinal column
14. brain

carefully pressing along the outsides of the sac with your thumb and forefinger positioned on either side of the gland. Be sure to hold a tissue below the gland to collect the fluid that flows out. If this procedure seems painful to the dog, or if there is any pus or blood mixed with the fluid, there is most likely an infection that will require veterinary attention.

The testicles should also be routinely inspected. An inflammation of the area, termed orchitis, may result from an injury to the testicle or an internal disorder. Left unchecked sterility can result. If the testicles appear enlarged, feel hard, or are painful for the dog (as evidenced by

Health Care

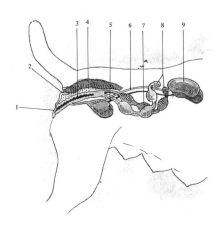

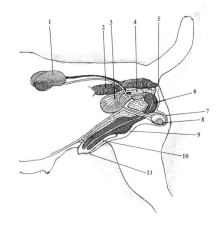

Reproductive system of the female:

1. vulva
2. anus
3. vagina
4. rectum
5. bladder

6. ureter
7. developing embryo
8. ovaries
9. kidneys

Reproductive system of the male:

1. kidneys
2. rectum
3. bladder
4. prostate
5. anus
6. urethra

7. scrotum
8. testes
9. bulb
10. penis
11. sheath

an unusual method of walking or sitting), immediate veterinary care is in order.

Hip Dysplasia

Although hip dysplasia (HD) is more commonly a disorder of the larger breeds, it does occasionally occur in some terrier breeds like the Airedale or giant and standard schnauzer. This disease is a congenital malformation of the hip joint that can finally lead to extreme pain when walking and sometimes leg paralysis for afflicted dogs. While steps can be taken to relieve the pain and slow the course of the disease, there is

no cure. Since the disease has been shown to be hereditary, at this time the best method for eliminating the problem is through a conscientious effort to breed only those dogs who do not show the disease or genetically carry a predisposition to it. If your breed has any tendency to HD and you intend to breed your terrier, both male and female should be x-rayed at approximately 12 to 15 months of age and the readings should be sent for evaluation by specialists from the Orthopedic Foundation for Animals (OFA). Only those animals that are certified as clear of hip dysplasia should be used in a breeding program.

Understanding Your Terrier

The Evolution of Dogs

The exact origin of the dog is unknown, but some theories place the first doglike animals on earth at around 600,000 B.C. Domesticated dogs are thought to date back about 20,000 years, with their closest recognizable ancestor the wolf. At a time when life was extremely harsh and food supplies limited, these primitive animals learned the benefits of grouping together for survival. Pack behavior developed, with the dogs assuming various ranks within the group. One dog assumed the leadership position, generally through an assertive show of power, and all pack members then worked out their own niche behind the leader.

In earliest times, human and dog competed for the same prey — and human intellect and superior skills ultimately won this contest. Dogs were intelligent enough to recognize, however, the benefits of adaptation to a secondary role as assistant. The dog's ability to subordinate itself to humans while still retaining its spirit has enabled the dog to become our favorite domesticated animal.

Early humans utilized dogs primarily to aid in the hunt for food; as time passed, people learned how to breed dogs selectively to attain certain goals: fast runners, good hunters, avid watchdogs. Such useful qualities served humans well. Over time a bond of friendship also arose and dual-purpose dogs arose: workers and companions.

Behavior Patterns and Their Meaning

While rarely called upon to activate their ancient survival instincts, modern dogs have nevertheless inherited many of the traits utilized by the earliest members of their species. Pack behavior still exists, but in modern times dogs adapt to the *human pack* and the additional demands of rules of civilization. Domestication has done much to temper the aggressive nature of many breeds, but many other characteristics have survived.

Terriers were originally bred to thrive predominantly in hilly territory and keep the terrain clear of predators and small vermin. In other terrains dogs of various structures and temperaments evolved to serve the particular needs of their masters. Even though raised as distinct breeds, they all share a common heritage and basic forms of communication.

Terriers are renowned for their spunky, aggressive nature. This trait is particularly keen in the males. When dog meets dog, there is an immediate vying for dominance. The dogs will stand well up on their feet, snarl, and try to intimidate their perceived opponent. An inspection of the anal area is generally in order. Fierce growling can ensue, and occasionally a fight will break out, but this is usually quite short-lived, as one animal will recognize its vulnerability and give way to the more dominant dog.

The same vying for top spot — the "alpha" dog — will also take place between dog and master, although this is more often a war of wits rather than a physical confrontation. Unless the human clearly asserts leadership, the dog feels it is entitled to rule the pack and will try to do so. Owners should be aware of this trait and exhibit an emphatic, consistent manner when dealing with the dog — especially when it willfully disobeys. The dog must understand that it is subordinate to all humans in its pack, and this instruction should begin as soon as the puppy is introduced into the household. A puppy can comprehend instruction in proper behavior even when quite young, as it has already been coached in this power structure by its mother, the original alpha.

Terriers are very alert, game animals. Despite their instinctive challenge to other animals they feel are vying for superior position, they are not normally prone to viciousness. The atrocities attributed to "pit bull terriers" are actions of poorly bred and improperly raised animals and should not be taken as typical of terrier nature. Owners of the larger, very game terrier breeds (American Staffordshire terrier, Staffordshire bull terrier) have an added responsibility to rigorously attend to obedience training of their animals, as the aggressive streak in such terriers must be tempered and properly channeled. By showing the public the attributes of well-bred, well-trained terriers, some of the ill fame attached to these breeds can be cleared away. As with all breeds, any terrier exhibiting an overly aggressive nature should be eliminated from breeding programs.

Vocalization, Facial Expression, and Posture

Body language and other nonverbal communication are basically uniform among all breeds of dogs — from the mighty mastiff to the diminutive Chihuahua. An Airedale will instinctively understand the significance of the posturing of the Great Dane, as well as the struts of the Yorkshire. Humans too can learn to interpret these body signs by paying attention to the differences among the various sounds dogs make, and the meaning of the accompanying movements.

A dog at ease will usually have a relaxed posture: the head and ears are up, the tail is at rest. When at attention, the ears point more forward, the tail is more horizontal, and the dog appears more up on its toes. When happy, as when greeting a familiar person, the tail usually moves quickly on a horizontal plane, the ears are up, and the dog may whine or give off some short barks. An upset, aggressive dog will have an angry expression, with its ears either pointed directly forward or lying flat against the side of the head, and it will begin to bare its teeth and emit low, growling tones.

A fearful dog is perhaps the most dangerous, as its agitation is not as apparent as a menacing animal's. It is highly unpredictable. The face is slightly tensed and the ears lie flat to the head; the overall body position is lowered. If the dog feels threatened, it can quickly lash out from this position.

Facial expressions are often keys to a dog's intent. This, however, can be complicated by the length and cut of a breed's coat around the face. Terriers such as the Yorkshires often have much of their face obscured by the lengthy coat, while Bedlingtons are trimmed to make them appear as lambs.

Tails are usually good mood indicators, but many of the terrier breeds have tails that are docked quite short, which makes monitoring the tail positions quite difficult. With dogs that have undocked tails, a horizontal position generally indicates contentment, an upward tail indicates excitement or heightened attention, and a low-slung tail position indicates fear.

Many people improperly interpret a dog's submissive posturing as an indication of guilt by the dog. This is, in fact, merely a resigned response by the dog to an authority more dominant that itself. A submissive dog assumes a lowered position, tail down and tucked under its belly, ears pointing back. It will avoid eye contact. In addition, it may attempt to lick the mouth or hands of the dominant individual. The dog may then roll onto its back or even urinate as further indication of its surrender.

A confused, upset dog may also assume a lowered stance, but it will not grovel or try to lick. Instead, its message is conveyed by rapid panting, indicative of stress.

Body language is highly revealing. By paying attention to your dog's signals, you should be able to assess a situation and make a proper response — such are the actions of a leader in the dog's view.

Communication

Communication with your dog is more than verbal exchanges — commands, praise, and corrections. To help mold your terrier puppy into a well-adjusted adult dog, there are a few basic concepts to bear in mind. A dog will respond to its master according to how it interprets that person's vocal tone and body language. This is all they have to work with. The master must, in turn, show the dog exactly what is expected of it.

Positive experiences teach your dog what you wish it to learn; negative experiences teach fear. A classic example of miscommunication is the following scenario: an owner discovers a housebreaking "mistake" on the carpet, screams in anger, even hits the dog, which is now crouched to the floor and scurrying for safe cover. The owner thinks the dog knows it has done wrong and is showing its guilt. The dog, in fact, is submitting to the master as a means of self-preservation. It hears and sees the anger and reacts with fear. The dog has not been helped to associate its actions with the master's reactions. This scenario is totally counterproductive; the dog is left confused and the owner has not taken the proper steps toward eliminating further such incidents.

A dog will learn *and retain* information gained from positive experiences. In theory, the learning process is quite simple: An effective leader clearly shows what is expected from the dog, and praises when the task is accomplished. If mistakes are made, the dog is corrected, shown the proper action, and praised when the action is finally completed.

This simple process can be complicated by many factors. Some terriers are more intelligent, capable learners. Some terriers are quite stubborn and less willing to submit to the will of the master. Some masters are better trainers. Each — dog and teacher — brings an individual set of strengths and weaknesses to the process, and a balance must be struck.

By being alert to what the dog's body language is telling you, and also to what *your* body language and vocal tones are telling the dog, communication can be improved. Your dog has a limited frame of reference, as it must rely on the signals you give with your vocal tones and physi-cal demeanor. If you encounter problems, try to use these cues to help evaluate what the cause may be: Is Rocco testing my authority? Is he confused? Am I making my wishes clear? Can Rocco attain what I am asking of him?

Digging and Burying

Terriers are earth dogs. While all dogs have been known to bury bones and leftover food as a throwback to the ancient times when this aided the dog's survival, this characteristic is deeply ingrained and must be expected in terriers. They love to dig, and many take to it with great fervor. Terriers make great use of their front paws, quickly burrowing deep into the ground, while the rear legs push the discarded dirt neatly (sometimes not so neatly) out the back.

The sheer joy of digging can be an annoyance for the owner. All fencing in the yard should be set to a depth that exceeds the digging capability of the dog, or the fence can be mounted in a solid foundation. Many terriers also display a curious habit of giving a quick dig in the immediate area where they are about to lie down; if this is your hardwood floor or carpeting, there is a problem. This is a throwback to the primitive times when the dog needed to carve out a nest for sleeping in order to protect itself from the elements. A firm, consistently repeated "no" at the instant the dog begins to scratch at the floor should solve this problem.

Most terriers will unhesitatingly enter into open holes or recesses; the possible danger of this is obvious. Do discourage this inclination and admonish the dog for crawling into tight spaces; the best course, however, is prevention. Be sure all old wells and drainage pipes are securely covered and impenetrable. If not, your terrier may take off after its prey—either real or imaginary—and end up wedged or injured.

Most of today's terrier breeds originated in the British Isles.

Understanding Your Terrier

Description of Terrier Breeds

Airedale Terrier

The Airedale is the largest member of the Terrier Group. It was developed in the 19th century by the sportsmen of Yorkshire to assist in hunting fox, badger, otter, and other small game that inhabited the area. The early Airedales were noted for their keen eyesight, hearing, agility, and courage, but fell short of the otter hound in scenting and swimming ability. During the early formative period these two breeds were occasionally crossed to improve the sporting abilities of both, and the result was a terrier of greater size and strength.

Over the years the Airedale has developed into a dog of many talents. It has been used in Africa to assist in big-game hunting, and was one of the first breeds used for police work. It excels as a companion and is noted for its loyalty, high-spirited nature, and protectiveness toward home and master. It has a warm, loving disposition, but can be aloof to strangers and other animals.

The Airedale sports a wiry, double coat and is tan with a black saddle. It is muscular, weighing from 45 to 60 pounds (20.4 kg–27.2 kg) on average, with an erect docked tail. The head is long and flat, with folded, V-shaped ears and dark, prominent eyes. Airedale litters range from five to ten puppies, with the newborns black at birth. The puppies develop the characteristic two-toned coat as they mature. The breed is quite hardy, although there is a tendency to hip dysplasia.

Because of its size and strength, the Airedale requires an outlet for its energies and should be given regular thorough workouts. While the breed is suitable for apartment living, the dog must also be given ample access to the outdoors.

To reach its fullest potential, the Airedale needs a lot of human contact and adequate discipline from an early age. Left to its own devices, the Airedale is willful enough to test the authority of its master, and must be reminded of its role as companion—not leader—in the household. Formal training in obedience methods is recommended. The Airedale thrives on human attention and develops a sweet disposition as it matures.

In the home the Airdale is a fine companion for all ages—strong and active enough to enjoy the rough play of youngsters and gentle enough to be trusted around small children. The Airedale is adaptable enough to accept other animals in the household, although it may be aggressive toward other male dogs.

The harsh, wiry coat of the Airedale must be combed and brushed several times a week and trimmed regularly to keep the dog looking tidy. Show dogs will require stripping and plucking, as clipping is not permissible and will damage

Airedale terriers, puppy and adult.

Note: **Standards for the terrier breeds appear with the permission of the American Kennel Club. For the full standard, including Faults and Disqualifications, see the AKC's Official Standards.**

the coat's desired texture. Bathing should be only as needed. During grooming and bathing inspect the skin for rashes or sores that might otherwise go undetected.

Official Standard for the Airedale Terrier

Head: Should be well balanced with little apparent difference between length of skull and foreface. *Skull* should be long and flat, not too broad between ears and narrowing very slightly to eyes. Scalp should be free from wrinkles, stop hardly visible and cheeks level and free from fullness. *Ears* should be V-shaped with carriage rather to side of head, not pointing to eyes, small but not out of proportion to size of dog. Topline of folded ear should be above level of skull. *Foreface* should be deep, powerful, strong, and muscular. Should be well filled up before eyes. *Eyes* should be dark, small, not prominent, full of terrier expression, keenness, and intelligence. *Lips* should be tight. *Nose* should be black and not too small. *Teeth* should be strong and white, free from discoloration or defect. Bite either level or viselike. A slightly overlapping or scissors bite is permissible without preference.

Neck: Should be of moderate length and thickness, gradually widening towards shoulders. Skin tight, not loose.

Shoulders and Chest: Shoulders long and sloping well into the back. Shoulder blades flat. From front, chest deep but not broad. Depth of chest should be approximately on a level with elbows.

Body: Back should be short, strong, and level. Ribs well sprung. Loins muscular and of good width. There should be but little space between last rib and hip joint.

Hindquarters: Should be strong and muscular with no droop.

Tail: Root of tail should be set well up on back. It should be carried gaily but not curled over back. It should be of good strength and substance and of fair length.

Legs: *Forelegs* should be perfectly straight, with plenty of muscle and bone. *Elbows* should be perpendicular to body, working free of sides. *Thighs* should be long and powerful with muscular second thigh, stifles well bent, not turned either in or out, hocks well let down, parallel with each other when viewed from behind. *Feet* should be small, round, and compact, with good depth of pad, well cushioned; toes moderately arched, not turned either in or out.

Coat: Should be hard, dense, and wiry, lying straight and close, covering dog well over body and legs. Some of the hardest are crinkling or just slightly waved. At the base of the hard very stiff hair should be a shorter growth of softer hair termed the undercoat.

Color: Head and ears should be tan, ears being of a darker shade than the rest. Dark markings on either side of skull are permissible. Legs up to thighs and elbows and underpart of the body and chest are also tan, and the tan frequently runs into the shoulder. Sides and upper parts of body should be black or dark grizzle. A red mixture is often found in the black and is not to be considered objectionable. Small white blaze on chest is a characteristic of certain strains of the breed.

Size: Dogs should measure approximately 23 inches (58.4 cm) in height at shoulder; bitches, slightly less. Both sexes should be sturdy, well muscled, and boned.

Movement: Movement or action is the crucial test of conformation. Movement should be free. As seen from the front, forelegs should swing perpendicular from body free from sides, feet the same distance apart as elbows. As seen from the rear the hind legs should be parallel with each other, neither too close nor too far apart, but so placed as to give a strong well-balanced stance and movement. Toes should not be turned either in or out.

Description of Terrier Breeds

American Staffordshire Terrier

Take just one look at a well-bred American Staffordshire terrier and the first impression will undoubtedly be one of strength and power. The breed dates to the late 19th century in the English countryside, where these dogs were developed to bait bulls. Dogfighting was also a popular "sport," and the ancestors of these dogs developed a reputation for unmatched courage, loyalty, and aggressiveness.

The early specimens—often called bull and terrier dogs or pit bull terriers—stemmed from bulldog and terrier crossings, with gameness the prime requirement. When dogfighting was outlawed, the breeding emphasis switched from ferocity to producing a dog extremely powerful for its size.

American Staffordshire terrier.

Over the years several different breeds developed from the early English stock: the American Staffordshire terrier, the Staffordshire bull terrier, and the bull terrier. The Staffordshire terrier specimens that found their way to America developed into a heavier, slightly larger type than the Staffordshire bull terrier in England, and the breeds were officially recognized as separate by the American Kennel Club in 1972.

Much has been written and said about the pit bull terrier in recent days, and to many people this term designates a vicious fighting dog. The American Staffordshire terrier suffers from this bad reputation. While a modern day American Staffordshire terrier is still a courageous dog, viciousness is not a typical trait. Poorly trained animals that stem from aggressive dogs of mixed lineage are generally responsible for the atrocities attributed to "pit bull terriers."

In appearance the breed is very powerfully built, with a short, sleek coat in any color but white that highlights its muscular body. It stands from 17 inches to 19 inches (43.2–48.3 cm) in height and weighs approximately 45 to 50 pounds (20.4–22.7 kg). The ears can be either cropped or uncropped, and the tail is low set and not docked.

The American Staffordshire terrier can be highly protective of its home and family, but is quite docile around the ones it loves. It does not care to share its home with another animal, but this and other game qualities can be moderated by obedience training, which is highly recommended. The breed is quite intelligent and takes well to such instruction. Its grooming requirements are minimal; routine brushing and an occasional bath (as needed) will generally suffice.

The Boston terrier, which was developed in the United States (top left). Handsome adult bull terriers (top right, bottom right), and a basketful of curious bull terrier puppies (bottom left).

Description of Terrier Breeds

This breed is not for everyone. It requires an experienced owner who can mold it into a loving companion by providing a substantial amount of vigorous exercise and competent obedience instruction.

Given adequate exercise, the American Staffordshire terrier is normally a hardy breed. There is a slight tendency toward hip dysplasia, and incidents of juvenile cataracts and immune system disorders have been noted. Litters average from five to ten puppies. Ear cropping is often performed by veterinarians when the puppies reach 12 weeks of age.

Official Standard for the American Staffordshire Terrier

General Impression: The American Staffordshire terrier should give the impression of great strength for his size, a well put-together dog, muscular, but agile and graceful, keenly alive to his surroundings. He should be stocky, not long-legged or racy in outline. His courage is proverbial.

Head: Medium length, deep through, broad skull, very pronounced cheek muscles, distinct stop; ears are set high. *Ears:* Cropped or uncropped, the latter preferred. Uncropped ears should be short and held half rose or prick. Full drop to be penalized. *Eyes:* Dark and round, low down in skull and set far apart. No pink eyelids. *Muzzle:* Medium length, rounded on upper side to fall away abruptly below eyes. Jaws well defined. Underjaw to be strong and have biting power. Lips close and even, no looseness. Upper teeth to meet tightly outside lower teeth in front. Nose definitely black.

Neck: Heavy, slightly arched, tapering from shoulders to back of skull. No looseness of skin. Medium length.

Shoulders: Strong and muscular with blades wide and sloping.

Back: Fairly short. Slight sloping from withers to rump with gentle short slope at rump to base of tail. Loins slightly tucked.

Body: Well-sprung ribs, deep in rear. All ribs close together. Forelegs set rather wide apart to permit chest development. Chest deep and broad.

Tail: Short in comparison to size, low set, tapering to a fine point; not curled or held over back. Not docked.

Legs: Front legs should be straight, large or round bones, pastern upright. No semblance of bend in front. Hindquarters well-muscled, let down at hocks, turning neither in nor out. Feet of moderate size, well arched and compact. Gait must be springy but without roll or pace.

Coat: Short, close, stiff to the touch, and glossy.

Color: Any color, solid, parti, or patched is permissible, but all white, more than 80% white, black and tan, and liver not to be encouraged.

Size: Height and weight should be in proportion. A height of about 18 to 19 inches (45.7–48.3 cm) at shoulders for the male and 17 to 18 inches (43.2–45.7 cm) for the female is to be considered preferable.

Staffordshire Bull terrier puppies (top left, bottom right) and adult (top right), and the somewhat larger American variety (bottom left).

Description of Terrier Breeds

Australian Terrier

Although developed in Australia during the 19th century, the Australian terrier has close ties to many of the short-legged terriers that hail from the United Kingdom. As colonists made their way "down under," they brought various types of terriers with them. It is believed that the breed is a result of crossings of the native rough-coat terrier with imported Dandie Dinmont, Cairn, Manchester, Irish, Skye, and possibly Yorkshire terrier strains.

Australian terriers, puppy and adult.

Australian fanciers were most interested in producing a small, hardy terrier that could serve as a companion in the home as well as an adept worker and hunter. Because of the harsh climate, the dog had to possess a rugged, easy-to-care-for coat that could protect the dog from the environment as well as from predators. The Australian excelled as a vermin and snake hunter, and was often used as guardian for the home and for livestock herds in the bushland.

The Australian terrier is one of the smallest of the working terriers, averaging about 10 inches (25.4 cm) in height and 12 to 14 pounds (5.4–6.3 kg) in weight, but its size does not prevent it from being one of the most energetic, outgoing terrier breeds. It is a very affectionate, personable dog that gets along well with everyone, including other dogs and house pets. The Australian is easy-going enough to be trusted around small children, yet game enough to serve as a reliable watchdog. It is very alert to all events in its home environment and quick to sound an alarm when strangers approach. Despite this vivacious spirit, the breed is generally quiet and relaxed around the home, not exhibiting any sign of hyperactivity.

This breed will thrive in any environment, in any size home, and needs only a moderate amount of exercise. The coat requires little more than a combing and brushing every few days to keep it looking neat. Shedding is minimal and bathing is needed infrequently. The long hairs that grow along the feet and ears, as well as any stray hairs in the coat, should be plucked for tidiness, but professional clipping is unnecessary. Inspect the skin frequently, however, since rashes can sometimes go unnoticed beneath the double coat; flea infestation can lead to serious irritations.

The Australian takes well to obedience training, which often helps to temper some of its exuberance. It is a very swift mover and should be kept on leash whenever outdoors to avoid a sudden dash into the path of danger.

Australian terrier litters are often quite small, averaging only three of four puppies, which are born almost completely black. They develop their tan markings as they age. The tail is docked to two-fifths length. The Australian terriers sport prick ears and a very keen expression.

Description of Terrier Breeds

Official Standard for the Australian Terrier

General Appearance: Small, sturdy, rough-coated terrier of spirited action and self-assured manner.
Head: Long, flat-skulled, and full between eyes, with stop moderate. Muzzle no longer than distance from eyes to occiput. Jaws long and powerful, teeth of good size, meeting in scissors bite, although level bite is acceptable. *Nose:* Black.
Ears: Set high on skull and well apart; small and pricked, the leather either pointed or slightly rounded and free from long hairs. *Eyes:* Small, dark, and keen in expression; not prominent.
Neck: Inclined to be long, tapering into sloping shoulders; well furnished with hair which forms a protective ruff.
Body: Low-set and slightly longer from withers to root of tail than from withers to ground. *Chest:* Medium wide, and deep, with ribs well sprung but not round. Topline level.
Tail: Set on high and carried erect but not too gay; docked leaving two fifths.
Legs and Feet: Forelegs straight and slightly feathered to carpus or so-called knee; set well under body with elbows close and pasterns strong. Hindquarters strong and well muscled but not heavy; legs moderately angulated at stifles and hocks, with hocks well let down. Bone medium in size. Feet small, clean, and catlike, toes arched and compact, nicely padded and free from long hair. Nails strong and black.
Coat: Outer coat harsh and straight, about two and one half inches all over body. Undercoat short and soft. Topknot, which covers only top of the skull, of finer texture and lighter color than body coat.
Color: May be blue-black or silver-black, with rich tan markings on head and legs, sandy color or clear red. The blue-black is bluish at roots and dark at tips. In silver-blacks each hair carries black and silver alternating with black at the tips. Tan is rich and deep, the richer the better. In sandies, any suggestion of smuttiness is undesirable.

Gait: Straight and true; sprightly, indicating spirit and assurance.
Temperament: That of a hard-bitten terrier, with aggressiveness of the natural ratter and hedge hunter, but as a companion, friendly, affectionate, and biddable.
Size: Shoulder height, about 10 inches (25.6 cm). Average weight 12 to 14 pounds (26.4–30.8 kg).

Bedlington Terrier

The Bedlington terrier is often compared in appearance to a lamb, with its light "fluffy" coat, hanging ears, and a docile expression. Appearances can be deceiving. The Bedlington terrier is a very game breed, is a swift, powerful runner, and an eager hunter of small and mid-size game. Its sense of hearing and sight are keen.

Bedlington terriers, puppy and adult.

Description of Terrier Breeds

The breed was developed early in the 19th century in the village of Bedlington in Northumberland, England. The Bedlington is believed to have been derived from the Dandie Dinmont terrier. Folklore has it that the Bedlingtons were used primarily by the gypsies of the Rothbury Forest, who trained the dogs to hunt the livestock of the rich landowners of the area. For a time, the breed was known as the Rothbury terrier.

The Bedlington terrier's high, arching back, attributed to crosses to sighthounds (probably whippets) in the formative days of the breed, enables it to run with great speed and have good endurance. Your Bedlington needs ample opportunity to exercise and run, but also exhibits a tendency to bolt and chase any moving object when allowed off leash, so be sure to have this terrier tethered when not in confined areas.

The lamblike appearance of the Bedlington is not easily achieved. The coat is nonshedding, comprised of a mixture of hard and soft hairs that stand out from the body. It takes regular, skillful trimming to get the desired look. The Bedlington terrier coat has a color range from sandy to liver. Litters range in size from three to six puppies; the colors of the newborns generally lighten as the dogs mature.

While the Bedlington is generally quite hardy, it has shown tendencies toward eye problems. In the home, this terrier is a loyal, loving companion when not threatened by the presence of other animals. The Bedlington's inclination to jealousy makes it less suited to homes with small, active children than other more docile terrier breeds. A stubborn streak is best tempered from your dog's earliest days in the home by adequate obedience training. This will also lay the groundwork for the tolerance a Bedlington needs for the grooming regimen.

Official Standard for the Bedlington Terrier

General Appearance: A graceful, lithe, well-balanced dog with no sign of coarseness, weakness or shelliness. In repose the expression is mild and gentle, not shy or nervous. Aroused, the dog is particularly alert and full of immense energy and courage. Noteworthy for endurance, Bedlingtons also gallop at great speed, as their body outline clearly shows.

Head: Narrow, but deep and rounded. Shorter in skull and longer in jaw. Covered with a profuse topknot lighter than color of body, highest at crown, and tapering gradually to just back of nose. There must be no stop and the unbroken line from crown to nose end reveals a slender head without cheekiness or snipiness. Lips black in the blue and tans and brown in all other solid and bicolors. *Eyes:* Almond-shaped, small, bright, and well sunk with no tendency to tear or water. Set is oblique and fairly high on head. Blues have dark eyes; blues and tans, less dark with amber lights; sandies, sandies and tans, light hazel; liver, livers and tans, slightly darker. Eye rims black in the blue and blue and tans, and brown in all other solid and bicolors. *Ears:* Triangular with rounded tips. Set on low and hanging flat to cheek in front with a slight projection at base. Point of greatest width approximately 3 inches (7.6 cm). Ear tips reach corners of mouth. Thin and velvety in texture, covered with fine hair forming a small silky tassel at the tip. *Nose:* Nostrils large and well defined. Blues and blues and tans have black noses. Livers, livers and tans, sandies, sandies and tans have brown noses. *Jaws:* Long and tapering. Strong muzzle well filled up with bone beneath eyes. Close-fitting lips, no flews. *Teeth:* Large, strong, and white. Level or scissors bite. Lower canines clasp outer surface of upper gum just in front of upper canines. Upper premolars and molars lie outside those of lower jaw.

Neck and Shoulders: Long, tapering neck with no throatiness, deep at base and rising well up from shoulders which are flat and sloping with no excessive musculature. Head is carried high.
Body: Muscular and markedly flexible. Chest deep. Flat-ribbed and deep through brisket, which reaches to elbows. Back has a good natural arch over loin, creating a definite tuck-up of the underline. Body slightly greater in length than height. Well-muscled quarters are also fine and graceful.
Legs and Feet: Lithe and muscular. Hind legs longer than forelegs, which are straight and wider apart at chest than at feet. Slight bend to pasterns which are long and sloping without weakness. Stifles well angulated. Hocks strong and well let down, turning neither in nor out. Long hare feet with thick, well-closed-up, smooth pads. Dewclaws should be removed.
Coat: A very distinctive mixture of hard and soft hair standing well out from the skin. Crisp to the touch but not wiry, having a tendency to curl, especially on the head and face. When in show trim must not exceed 1 inch (2.5 cm) on body; hair on legs slightly longer.
Tail: Set low, scimitar-shaped, thick at root and tapering to a point which reaches hock. Not carried over back or tight to underbody.
Color: Blue, sandy, liver, blue and tan, sandy and tan, liver and tan. In bicolors tan markings are found on legs, chest, under tail, inside hindquarters, and over each eye. Topknots of all adults should be lighter than body color. Patches of darker hair from an injury are not objectionable, as these are only temporary. Darker body pigmentation of all colors is to be encouraged.
Height: The preferred Bedlington terrier dog measures 16½ inches (42.0 cm) at withers; bitch 15½ inches (39.4 cm). Under 16 inches (41.0 cm) or over 17½ inches (43.2 cm) for dogs and under 15 inches (38.1 cm) or over 16½ inches (42.0 cm) for bitches are serious faults.

Weight: To be proportionate to height within the range of 17 to 23 pounds (7.7–10.4 kg).
Gait: Unique lightness of movement. Springy in slower paces, not stilted or hackneyed. Must not cross, weave, or paddle.

Border Terrier

The border terrier evolved from various terrier strains that were found in the hill country of England in the area that *borders* Scotland. This hardy working terrier was unmatched in its ability to seek out and kill the predators of the local livestock, and it was admired for being able to subdue even the more vicious animals through a combination of courage, stamina, and cunning.

Border terrier.

In appearance, the border terrier is often described as "plain." It stands approximately 12 to 13 inches (30.7–33.3 cm) in height, has a wiry double coat, an erect, undocked tail, and a head that is said to resemble an otter's. While it is one of the smaller terriers, it is very capable. It takes easily and naturally to the hunt, yet is a bit more even-tempered than many of the feisty terrier breeds.

In the home the border terrier is a well-mannered companion that makes little demand on its owners. In personality, the border terrier is often described as "pleasant." Its coat is almost maintenance-free and seldom requires more than an occasional brushing and some limited trimming to keep stray hairs neat. It does require some vigorous exercise each day, as it has a lot of energy despite its small frame. The border terrier is quite sensitive to what is going on around it at all times, so it is advisable to keep it on leash when out walking, as it may be inclined to bolt after any small animal that it spies in the distance.

One of the more docile terriers, the border breed fits well into the home. It is happy to serve as companion in an apartment setting, yet adapts well to a more rugged environment that includes small children and other pets. Its strong will is easily tempered by obedience lessons, which the dog takes to quite readily.

The border terrier is generally a very healthy and long-lived breed with no notable health problems. There are usually no breeding or whelping difficulties, and litters commonly range in size from three to six. It is found in a number of colors (red, tan, wheaten), with newborns of various colors found in the same litter.

The border terrier is a fine example of the true terrier. It has not been extensively refined over the years and remains today much like the early representatives of the breed. It is unspoiled, unpampered, and uninhibited.

Official Standard for the Border Terrier

Since the border terrier is a working terrier of a size to go to ground and able, within reason, to follow a horse, his conformation should be such that he be ideally built to do his job. No deviations from this ideal conformation should be permitted, which would impair his usefulness in running his quarry to earth and in bolting it therefrom. For this work he must be alert, active, and agile, and capable of squeezing through narrow apertures and rapidly traversing any kind of terrain. His head, "like that of an otter," is distinctive, and his temperament ideally exemplifies that of a terrier. By nature he is good-tempered, affectionate, obedient, and easily trained. In the field he is hard as nails, "game as they come," and driving in attack. It should be the aim of border terrier breeders to avoid such overemphasis of any point in the Standard as might lead to unbalanced exaggeration.

General Appearance: An active terrier of medium bone, strongly put together, suggesting endurance and agility, but rather narrow in shoulder, body, and quarter. Body is covered with a somewhat broken though close-fitting and intensely wiry jacket. The characteristic "otter" head with its keen eye, combined with a body poise which is "at the alert," gives a look of fearless and implacable determination characteristic of the breed. Proportions should be that height at withers is slightly greater than the distance from withers to tail, *i.e.,* by possibly 1–1½ inches (2.5–3.8 cm) in a 14-pound (30.8 kg) dog.

Weight: Dogs, 13–15½ pounds (28.6–34.1 kg), bitches, 11½–14 pounds (25.3–30.8 kg), are appropriate weights for border terriers in hard-working condition.

Head: Similar to that of an otter. Moderately broad and flat in skull with plenty of width between eyes and between ears. Slight, moderately broad curve at stop rather than a pronounced in-

Description of Terrier Breeds

dentation. Cheeks slightly full. *Ears:* Small, V-shaped and of moderate thickness, dark preferred. Not set high on head but somewhat on the side, and dropping forward close to cheeks. They should not break above level of skull. *Eyes:* Dark hazel and full of fire and intelligence. Moderate in size, neither prominent nor small and beady. *Muzzle:* Short and "well filled." A dark muzzle is characteristic and desirable. A few short whiskers are natural to the breed. *Teeth:* Strong, with a scissors bite, large in proportion to size of dog. *Nose:* Black, and of a good size.

Neck: Clean, muscular and only long enough to give well-balanced appearance. It should gradually widen into shoulder. *Shoulders:* Well laid back and of good length, blades converging to withers gradually from brisket not excessively deep or narrow.

Forelegs: Straight and not too heavy in bone and placed slightly wider than in a fox terrier. *Feet:* Small and compact. Toes should point forward and be moderately arched with thick pads.

Body: Deep, fairly narrow and of sufficient length to avoid any suggestions of lack of range and agility. Deep ribs carried well back and not oversprung in view of desired depth and narrowness of body. Body should be capable of being spanned by a man's hands behind the shoulders. Back strong but laterally supple, with no suspicion of dip behind shoulder. Loin strong and underline fairly straight.

Tail: Moderately short, thick at base, then tapering. Not set on too high. Carried gaily when at the alert, but not over back. When at ease, a border may drop his stern.

Hindquarters: Muscular and racy, with thighs long and nicely molded. Stifles well bent and hocks well let down.

Coat: A short and dense undercoat covered with a very wiry and somewhat broken top coat which should lie closely, but must not show any tendency to curl or wave. With such a coat a border

should be able to be exhibited almost in his natural state, nothing more in the way of trimming being needed than a tidying-up of head, neck and feet. *Hide:* Very thick and loose fitting.

Movement: Straight and rhythmical before and behind, with good length of stride and flexing of stifle and hock. Dog should respond to his handler with a gait which is free, agile and quick.

Color: Red, grizzle and tan, blue and tan, or wheaten. A small amount of white may be allowed on chest but white on feet should be penalized.

Boston Terrier

At the beginning of the 20th century, the Boston terrier was the most popular purebred dog in America. It boasts an affectionate nature, a lively personality, and a sociable outlook. It relishes the role of house pet, as it loves the company of children, adults, and even other pets. It will thrive in any environment, from city apartment to the country. This terrier is very alert to everything that goes on around it and is a natural watchdog.

The Boston terrier is one of the few breeds actually developed in the United States, and its name attests to its homeland. It was originated by crossing terrier strains descended from the English terrier with various types of bulldogs. Over the years it was slowly downgraded in size from an average of 35 pounds (15.9 kg) in the 19th century to its current weight of 15 to 25 pounds (6.8–11.3 kg). It averages about 17 inches (43.2 cm) in height and has a very short, square muzzle and large, round eyes. The preferred color is a brindle with white markings on the face, forehead, breast, and forelegs.

The Boston terrier is assigned to the Non-sporting Group rather than the Terrier Group, as the breed was never intended as an earth dog; it lacks much of the game, aggressive nature typi-

Description of Terrier Breeds

Boston terriers, puppy and adult.

cal of many of the terrier breeds. It does have a streak of stubbornness, however, that should be tempered by obedience training. Training the Boston terrier to the rules of the household should be easily accomplished, as this is a very intelligent breed. It takes well to any type of home, and requires little more than a daily walk. An occasional grooming with a bristle brush or grooming glove is all that is needed to keep the coat smooth and shiny.

Because of its short muzzle, the Boston terrier is often prone to respiratory ailments, and it may also snore and wheeze. Its eyes are easily injured and it is subject to skin ailments and tumors. The large head also often impedes normal delivery, so cesarean sections are common. Litters gener-

ally contain from three to five puppies, which become very active at a very early age and will need an early introduction to obedience training.

Official Standard for the Boston Terrier

General Appearance: Should be that of a lively, highly intelligent, smooth-coated, short-headed, compactly built, short-tailed, well-balanced dog of medium station, of brindle color, and evenly marked with white. Head should indicate a high degree of intelligence, and should be in proportion to size of dog; body rather short and well knit, limbs strong and neatly turned; tail short; no feature so prominent that dog appears badly proportioned. Dog should convey an impression of determination, strength, and activity, with style of a high order; carriage easy and graceful. A proportionate combination of "color" and "ideal markings" is a particularly distinctive feature of a representative specimen, and a dog with a preponderance of white on body, or without the proper proportion of brindle and white on head, should possess sufficient merit otherwise to counteract its deficiencies in these respects. The ideal "Boston terrier expression" as indicating "a high degree of intelligence," is also an important characteristic of the breed. "Color and markings" and "expression" should be given particular consideration in determining the relative value of "general appearance" to other points.

Skull: Square, flat on top, free from wrinkles; cheeks flat; brow abrupt, stop well defined. *Eyes:* Wide apart, large and round, dark in color, expression alert, but kind and intelligent. Eyes should set square in skull, and outside corners should be on a line with cheeks as viewed from front. *Muzzle:* Short, square, wide and deep, and in proportion to skull; free from wrinkles; shorter in length than in width and depth, not exceeding in length approximately one third of length of skull; width and depth carried out well to end; muzzle from stop to end of nose on a line parallel to top of skull; nose black and wide, with well-defined line between nostrils. Jaws broad and square, with short regular teeth. Bite even or sufficiently undershot to square muzzle. Chops of good depth not pendulous, completely covering teeth when mouth is closed. *Ears:* Carried erect, either cropped to conform to shape of head, or natural bat, situated as near corners of skull as possible.

Neck: Of fair length, slightly arched and carrying head gracefully; setting neatly into shoulders.

Body: Deep with good width of chest; shoulders sloping; back short; ribs deep and well sprung, carried well back to loins; loins short and muscular; rump curving slightly to set-on of tail; flank very slightly cut up. Body should appear short but not chunky.

Elbows: Standing neither in nor out. *Forelegs:* Set moderately wide apart and on line with point of shoulders; straight in bone and well muscled; pasterns short and strong. *Hind Legs:* Set true; bent at stifles; short from hocks to feet; hocks turning neither in nor out; thighs strong and well muscled. *Feet:* Round, small and compact and turned neither in nor out; toes well arched.

Gait: That of a sure-footed, straight-gaited dog, forelegs and hind legs moving straight ahead in line with perfect rhythm, each step indicating grace with power.

Tail: Set-on low; short, fine and tapering; straight; or screw; devoid of fringe or coarse hair, and not carried above horizontal.

Ideal Color: Brindle with white markings. Brindle to be evenly distributed and distinct. Black with white markings permissible but brindle with white markings preferred. *Ideal Markings:* White muzzle, even white blaze over head, collar, breast, part or whole of forelegs, and hind legs below hocks.

Coat: Short, smooth, bright, and fine in texture.

Weight: Not exceeding 25 pounds (11.3 kg), divided by classes as follows: lightweight, under 15 pounds (6.8 kg); middleweight, 15 to 20 pounds (6.8–9.1 kg); heavyweight, 20 to 25 pounds (9.1–11.3 kg).

Bull Terrier

Many newcomers to this breed are surprised to discover that the bull terrier can be as gentle and loving as it is rugged looking. The breed's powerful build is highlighted by big-boned legs, muscular shoulders, and a well-rounded chest. The head is oval, with small, deeply set eyes that give the face a look of intelligence and confidence.

Bull terriers, puppy and adult.

Description of Terrier Breeds

The bull terrier was devised in 19th-century England primarily for the purpose of dogfighting. Breeders crossed the bulldog of that time with a very game dog from the area called the English terrier, to produce a dog with the strength and endurance of the former and the speed and punishing bite of the latter. Once dogfighting was abolished, the breed remained quite popular because of its unsurpassed loyalty to owner and home.

While it is obvious that the bull terrier is not the breed for everyone, it is very amiable, people-oriented. It is a quick learner with very clean habits and mannerisms. The owner must be assertive with a bull terrier right from the start; more than elementary obedience training is required. With such guidance the bull terrier will mature into an excellent companion. The bull terrier does best in a single-pet household, as it is often not tolerant of other animals. Because of its assertive nature, this breed should never be allowed to roam the neighborhood unsupervised, since once challenged it will not avoid a fight. It may also view any animal that enters its territory as an intruder. The bull terrier needs an outlet for its energy and will require at least one long walk daily. A twice-weekly grooming with a hound glove or bristle brush is all that is needed to keep the bull terrier looking neat. Bathe these dogs only when necessary. All-white dogs naturally show dirt more than colored ones, and may require more cleanup if allowed much time outdoors.

The bull terrier usually weighs 50 to 60 pounds (22.7–27.2 kg) and stands approximately 22 inches (56.0 cm) high. Its coat is short, glossy, and harsh to the touch, with various colors permissible. These include solid white, white with markings on the head, and brindled. Aside from a slight tendency for all-white bull terriers to have hearing problems, the breed is exceptionally hardy. Litters typically contain four to eight puppies, with a variety of colors possible in every litter. No whelping problems are common.

Official Standard for the Bull Terrier
WHITE

The Bull Terrier must be strongly built, muscular, symmetrical and active, with a keen determined and intelligent expression, full of fire but of sweet disposition and amenable to discipline.

Head: Should be long, strong and deep right to end of muzzle, but not coarse. Full face should be oval in outline and be filled completely up giving the impression of fullness with a surface devoid of hollows or indentations, *i.e.*, egg shaped. In profile it should curve gently downwards from top of skull to tip of nose. Forehead should be flat across from ear to ear. Distance from tip of nose to eyes should be perceptibly greater than that from eyes to top of skull. Underjaw should be deep and well defined. *Lips* should be clean and tight. *Teeth* should meet in either a level or scissors bite. In scissors bite upper teeth should fit in front of and closely against lower teeth, and they should be sound, strong, and perfectly regular. *Ears* should be small, thin and placed close together. Should be capable of being held stiffly erect, when they should point upwards. *Eyes* should be well sunken and as dark as possible, with a piercing glint and they should be small, triangular, and obliquely placed; set near together and high up on dog's head. Blue eyes are a disqualification. *Nose* should be black, with well-developed nostrils bent downward at tip.

Neck: Should be very muscular, long, arched and clean, tapering from shoulders to head and it should be free of loose skin.

Chest: Should be broad when viewed from front, and there should be great depth from withers to brisket, so that the latter is nearer the ground than the belly.

Body: Should be well rounded with marked spring of rib; back should be short and strong. Back ribs deep. Slightly arched over loin. Shoulders should be strong and muscular but without heaviness. Shoulder blades should be wide and flat and there should be a very pronounced backward slope from bottom edge of blade to top edge. Behind shoulders there should be no slackness or dip at withers. Underline from brisket to belly should form a graceful upward curve.

Legs: Should be big boned but not to the point of coarseness; forelegs should be of moderate length, perfectly straight; dog must stand firmly upon them. Elbows must turn neither in nor out; pasterns should be strong and upright. Hind legs should be parallel viewed from behind. Thighs very muscular with hocks well let down. Hind pasterns short and upright. Stifle joint should be well bent with a well-developed second thigh. *Feet* round and compact with well-arched toes like a cat.

Tail: Should be short, set on low, fine, and ideally should be carried horizontally. Should be thick where it joins body, and should taper to a fine point.

Coat: Should be short, flat, harsh to the touch, and with a fine gloss. Skin should fit tightly. *Color* is white though markings on head are permissible. Any markings elsewhere on coat are to be severely faulted. Skin pigmentation not to be penalized.

Movement: Dog shall move smoothly, covering ground with free, easy strides, fore and hind legs should move parallel each to each when viewed from in front or behind. Forelegs reaching out well and hind legs moving smoothly at hip and flexing well at stifle and hock. Dog should move compactly and in one piece but with a typical jaunty air that suggests agility and power.

COLORED

The standard for the colored variety is the same as for the white except for the subhead "Color" which reads: *Color.* Any color other than white, or any color with white markings. Other things being equal, the preferred color is brindle. A dog which is predominantly white shall be disqualified.

Cairn Terrier

The cairn is thought to be one of the oldest terrier breeds, dating back hundreds of years to its homeland on Britain's Isle of Skye. This terrier's task was always to hunt out the predators that stalked and hid in the "cairns" or rock piles of this area's rugged terrain. This was a job requiring skill, nimbleness, stamina, and a superior terrier gameness, and the cairn terrier earned a reputation for steadfastness against any obstacle.

The cairn terrier also earned high praise as a companion in the home, for it blended a strong sense of loyalty with a wariness of strangers, making it a natural watchman over home and children. The cairn is very affectionate toward its loved ones, and is more outgoing and good-natured than many other terriers who sometimes become snappy when subjected to the rough-housing of children. Cairns take such tumult in stride and can often outlast the seemingly endless energy of children.

Cairn terriers, puppy and adult.

Description of Terrier Breeds

A cairn terrier goes about anything it undertakes with zeal. It is a very rugged and hardy breed, often living well into the teens. Its hard, weather-resistant coat requires only a moderate amount of grooming to keep it tidy. Its exercise requirements are not excessive, but it does enjoy as much activity as it can have. This does not, however, mean that the cairn is not suited for a sedate household. This terrier gets along well in almost every situation, matching its daily activities to its master's schedule and interests.

Litters average three to five puppies, which can be any color but white. They housetrain easily. Cairns are very intelligent and can become a bit devious if allowed to rule their home without restrictions, so basic obedience training is suggested. Like almost every true terrier, the cairn will follow its instincts and bolt after any small animal that appears, so be sure to keep the dog on leash when not in a fenced lot.

The cairn is one of the most cherished house pets among the terrier breeds. Its personality is all but faultless: pleasant, loving, happy, devoted. There is a lot of dog in this small frame.

Official Standard for the Cairn Terrier

General Appearance: That of an active, game, hardy, small working terrier of the short-legged class; very free in its movements, strongly but not heavily built, standing well forward on its forelegs, deep in the ribs, well coupled with strong hindquarters and presenting a well-proportioned build with a medium length of back, having a hard, weather-resisting coat; head shorter and wider than any other terrier and well furnished with hair giving a general foxy expression.

Head: *Skull:* Broad in proportion to length with a decided stop and well furnished with hair on top of head, which may be somewhat softer than body coat. *Muzzle:* Strong but not too long or heavy. *Teeth:* Large, mouth neither overshot nor undershot. *Nose:* Black. *Eyes:* Set wide apart, rather sunken, with shaggy eyebrows, medium in size, hazel or dark hazel in color, depending on body color, with a keen terrier expression. *Ears:* Small, pointed, well carried erectly, set wide apart on side of head. Free from long hairs.

Tail: In proportion to head, well furnished with hair but not feathery. Carried gaily but must not curl over back. Set on at back level.

Body: Well-muscled, strong, active body with well-sprung, deep ribs, coupled to strong hindquarters, with level back of medium length, giving an impression of strength and activity without heaviness.

Shoulders, Legs and Feet: Sloping shoulder, medium length of leg, good but not too heavy bone; forelegs should not be out at elbows, and be perfectly straight, but forefeet may be slightly turned out. Forefeet larger than hind feet. Legs must be covered with hard hair. Pads should be thick and strong and dog should stand well up on its feet.

Coat: Hard and weather-resistant. Must be double-coated with profuse harsh outer coat and short, soft, close, furry undercoat.

Color: May be any color except white. Dark ears, muzzle, and tail tip are desirable.

Ideal Size: Involves weight, height at withers and length of body. Weight for bitches, 13 pounds (5.9 kg); for dogs, 14 pounds (6.4 kg). Height at withers—bitches, 9½ inches (24.1 cm); dogs, 10 inches (25.4 cm). Length of body from 14½ to 15 inches (36.8–38.1 cm) from front of chest to back of hindquarters. Must be of balanced proportions and appear neither leggy nor too low to ground; neither too short nor too long in body. Weight and measurements are for matured dogs at two years of age. Older dogs may weigh slightly in excess and growing dogs may be under these weights and measurements.

Condition: Dogs should be shown in good hard flesh, well muscled and neither too fat nor too thin. Should be in full good coat with plenty of head furnishings, be clean, combed, brushed, and tidied up on ears, tail, feet, and general outline. Should move freely and easily on a loose lead, should not cringe on being handled, should stand up on their toes, and show with marked terrier characteristics.

Dandie Dinmont Terrier

The Dandie Dinmont terrier is a "Scottish" type of terrier. It is very short in the leg and long in the body, but has pendulous ears—a trait that came late to the terriers of Scotland. The breed is thought to be related to the other terriers that hail from this area of the British Isles, the border and Bedlington terriers.

Dandie Dinmont terrier.

The breed attracted much attention with the publication of *Guy Mannering*, by Sir Walter Scott. In this novel a character named Dandie Dinmont had two feisty terriers of pepper and mustard coloring that excelled not only as vermin hunters but as intelligent, loyal companions.

The breed traces its name to this fictional character, who did much to popularize a breed that had previously been confined to the wilds of Scotland.

The Dandie Dinmont terrier is a very game dog, prone to challenging other animals—whether a predatory fox or another dog (especially males). If this tendency is not tempered from youth, the Dandie will be unruly around other animals as an adult. Obedience training is a must, as is a leash at all times when the dog is outdoors. It is often an extraordinary digger. The Dandie can be quite stubborn, so be patient and firm if it should rebel.

The typical height for a Dandie Dinmont is 8 to 11 inches (20.3–28.0 cm) at the top of the shoulder, and it weighs from 18 to 24 pounds (8.2–10.9 kg). Litters generally contain three to six puppies, and maturity comes late to the breed. The adult coat color will normally be set by about eight months of age, but it will take two to three years for the dog to reach physical maturity.

The Dandie Dinmont is a hardy breed that can withstand a rigorous lifestyle with no apparent stress, although having to climb stairs may cause back problems for susceptible dogs. The coat is about 2 inches (5.1 cm) in length, with a mixture of hard and soft hairs. Grooming requirements are moderate, as it sheds little, but a brushing every other day is recommended to keep the hair from matting. Clipping, required to keep the typical Dandie look, is best handled by a professional. A moderate amount of exercise is advisable, but the Dandie can be kept in an urban setting without problem.

The Dandie Dinmont is a sensible house pet. It learns household manners fairly quickly and generally does not act up unless provoked. It is quite intelligent, paying close attention to what goes on around it. Its loyalty is intense. Should the circumstances arise, a Dandie Dinmont might not take well to a new home once original attachments have been made.

Description of Terrier Breeds

Official Standard for the Dandie Dinmont Terrier

Head: Strongly made and large, not out of proportion to dog's size, muscles showing extraordinary development, more especially the maxillary. *Skull* broad between ears, getting gradually less towards eyes, and measuring about the same from inner corner of eye to back of skull as it does from ear to ear. Forehead well domed. Head *covered* with very soft silky hair, which should not be confined to a mere topknot, and the lighter in color and silkier it is the better. *Cheeks,* starting from ears proportionately with skull have a gradual taper towards muzzle, which is deep and strongly made, and measures about 3 inches (7.6 cm) in length, or in proportion to skull as 3 is to 5. *Muzzle* is covered with hair of a little darker shade than topknot, and of the same texture as feather of forelegs. Top of muzzle generally bare for about an inch (2.5 cm) from back part of nose, the bareness coming to a point towards eye, and being about one inch (2.5 cm) broad at the nose. *Nose* and inside of *Mouth* black or dark-colored. *Teeth* very strong, especially canines, which are of extraordinary size for a small dog. Canines mesh well with each other, so as to give greatest available holding and punishing power. Incisors in each jaw are evenly spaced and six in number, with upper incisors overlapping lower incisors in a tight, scissors bite. *Eyes:* Set wide apart, large, full, round, bright, expressive of great determination, intelligence, and dignity; set low and prominent in front of head; color, a rich dark hazel. *Ears:* Pendulous, set well back, wide apart, and low on skull, hanging close to cheek, with a very slight projection at the base, broad at junction of head and tapering almost to a point, forepart of ear tapering very little—tapering mostly on back part, forepart of ear coming almost straight down from its junction with head to tip. They should harmonize in color with body color. In a pepper dog they are covered with a soft straight brownish hair (in some cases almost black). In a mustard dog hair should be mustard in color, a shade darker than body, but not black. All should have a thin feather of light hair starting about 2 inches (5.1 cm) from tip, and of nearly the same color and texture as topknot, which gives ear the appearance of a *distinct point*. Animal is often 1 or 2 years old before feather is shown. Cartilage and skin of ear should not be thick, but rather thin. Length of ear from 3 to 4 inches (7.6–10.2 cm).

Neck: Very muscular, well-developed, and strong, showing great power of resistance, well set into shoulders.

Body: Long, strong, and flexible; ribs well sprung and round, chest well developed and let well down between forelegs; back rather low at shoulder, having a slight downward curve and a corresponding arch over loins, with a very slight gradual drop from top of loins to root of tail; both sides of backbone well supplied with muscle.

Tail: Rather short, say from 8 to 10 inches (20.5–25.6 cm) and covered on upper side with wiry hair of darker color than that of body, hair on underside lighter in color and not so wiry, with nice feather about 2 inches (5.1 cm) long, getting shorter as it nears tip; rather thick at root, getting thicker for about 4 inches (10.2 cm), then tapering off to a point. Should not be twisted or curled in any way, but should come up with a curve like a scimitar; tip, when excited, in a perpendicular line with root of tail. Should be set on neither too high nor too low. When not excited it is carried gaily, a little above level of body.

Legs: Forelegs short, with immense muscular development and bone, set wide apart, chest coming well down between them. Feet well formed *and not flat*, with very strong brown or dark-colored claws. Bandy legs and flat feet are objectionable. Hair on forelegs and feet of a pepper dog should be tan, varying according to body color from a rich tan to a pale fawn; of a mustard dog a darker shade than its head, which is a creamy white. In both colors there is a nice feather, about 2 inches (5.1 cm) long, rather lighter in color than hair on forepart of leg. Hind legs a little longer than forelegs, and set rather wide apart but not spread out in an unnatural manner, while feet are much smaller; thighs are well developed, and hair of same color and texture as forelegs, but having no feather or dew-claws; whole claws should be dark; but claws of all vary in shade according to color of body.

Coat: A very important point; hair should be about 2 inches (5.1 cm) long; that from skull to root of tail, a mixture of hardish and soft hair, which gives a sort of crisp feel to the hand. The hard should not be wiry; coat is what is termed piley or penciled. Hair on underpart of body is lighter in color and softer than on top. Skin on belly accords with color of dog.

Color: Pepper or mustard. Pepper ranges from dark bluish black to light silvery gray, intermediate shades preferred, body color coming well down shoulder and hips, gradually merging into leg color. Mustards vary from reddish brown to pale fawn, head a creamy white, legs and feet a shade darker than head. Claws are dark as in other colors. (Nearly all Dandie Dinmont terriers have some white on chest, and some also have white claws.)

Size: Height should be from 8 to 11 inches (20.3–28.0 cm) at top of shoulder. Length from top of shoulder to root of tail should not be more than twice the dog's height, but preferably 1 or 2 inches (2.5 or 5 cm) less.

Weight: Preferred weight from 18 to 24 pounds (8.2–10.9 kg). These weights are for dogs in good working condition.

Fox Terrier (Smooth, Wire, and Toy)

The smooth and wire fox terriers date back to the mid-1800s; they were developed by hunt masters who required the services of a game, compact dog to flush the fox once it had gone to earth. The two breeds are now accepted by the American Kennel Club as distinct breeds, with the only

Fox terriers, wire adult (left); smooth adult and wire puppy (right).

true difference being the coat. The toy fox terrier was developed in the 1920s from selective breedings of small smooth fox terrier specimens. Because of its diminutive size, the toy fox terrier has come to serve primarily as a companion.

The standard size smooth and fox terrier averages from 16 to 18 pounds (7.3–8.2 kg) and stands up to 15$\frac{1}{2}$ inches (39.4 cm) at the withers.

Description of Terrier Breeds

The toy averages from 3 to 7 pounds (1.4–3.2 kg) and can be up to 10 inches (25.4 cm) at the withers. All sport a muscular, well-contoured body.

The fox terrier is a people-oriented dog that makes a welcome house pet. It is friendly and personable, with a desire to get in on all the happenings of the family rather than watch from the sidelines. Regardless of type or size, the fox terrier is a natural watchdog, and even may go a bit too far by being an overly vocal dog. With a little training, the fox terrier can master any number of tricks and has often been used as a circus performer. It is an energetic dog that enjoys an active lifestyle. While the breed can do well with elderly or sedentary owners, it does best with those who can put it through its paces, such as a family with children.

The smooth and toy fox terriers require little more than an occasional brushing with a hound glove or bristle brush to keep the coat shiny and healthy. The wire fox terrier requires more attention. A show dog will need to have its coat regularly stripped and plucked to maintain proper texture and tidiness. A pet wire fox terrier may be clipped to maintain a neat appearance, but this will somewhat soften the coat from the ideal texture described in the breed standard; this does not, however, present any health risks.

Fox terriers are hardy dogs, but can be subject to eye and ear problems. Wire and smooth bitches generally have few whelping difficulties; their litters usually contain from three to six puppies. Toy fox terriers can be prone to whelping problems because of their size; their litters usually contain two or three puppies.

Official Standard for the Smooth Fox Terrier

Head: Skull should be flat and moderately narrow, gradually decreasing in width to eyes. Not much "stop" should be apparent, but there should be more dip in profile between forehead and top jaw than is seen in a greyhound. *Cheeks* must not be full. *Ears* should be V-shaped and small, of moderate thickness, and drooping forward close to cheek, not hanging by side of head like a foxhound. Top line of folded ear should be well above level of skull. *Jaws*, upper and lower, should be strong and muscular and of fair punishing strength, but not so as in any way to resemble the greyhound or modern English terrier. There should not be much falling away below eyes. This part of head should, however, be moderately chiseled out, so as not to go down in a straight slope like a wedge. *Nose*, towards which muzzle must gradually taper, should be black. It should be noticed that although foreface should gradually taper from eye to muzzle and should tip slightly at its junction with forehead, it should not "dish" or fall away quickly below eyes, where it should be full and well made up, but relieved from "wedginess" by a little delicate chiseling. *Eyes* and the *Rims* should be dark, moderately small and rather deep set, full of fire, life, and intelligence, and as nearly possible circular. Anything approaching a yellow eye is most objectionable. *Teeth* should be as nearly as possible together, i.e., points of upper (incisor) teeth on outside of or slightly overlapping lower teeth. There should be apparent little difference in length between skull and foreface of a well-balanced head.

The sprightly fox terrier (top) and Jack Russell terrier (bottom). The latter is not yet an officially recognized breed.

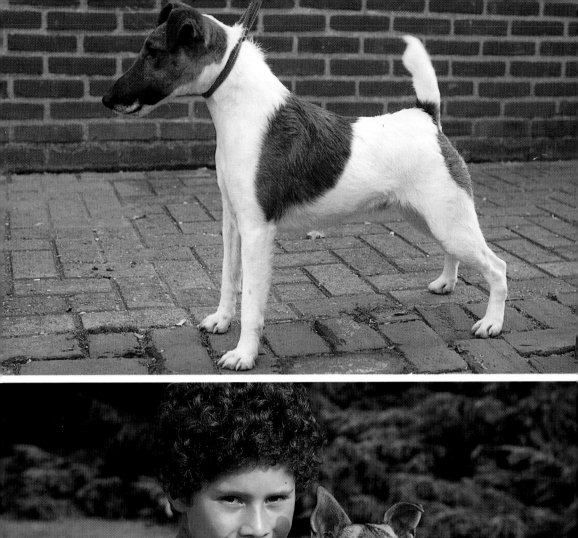

Description of Terrier Breeds

Neck: Should be clean and muscular, without throatiness, of fair length, and gradually widening to shoulders.

Shoulders: Should be long and sloping, well laid back, fine at points, and clearly cut at withers.

Chest: Deep and not broad.

Back: Should be short, straight, (i.e., level), and strong, with no appearance of slackness. *Brisket* should be deep, yet not exaggerated. *Loin* should be very powerful, muscular, and very slightly arched. Foreribs should be moderately arched, back ribs deep and well sprung, and dog should be well ribbed up.

Hindquarters: Should be strong and muscular, quite free from droop or crouch; thighs long and powerful, stifles well curved and turned neither in nor out; hocks well bent and near the ground should be perfectly upright and parallel each with the other when viewed from behind, dog standing well up on them like a foxhound, and not straight in stifle. Worst possible form of hindquarters consists of short second thigh and straight stifle.

Stern: Should be set on rather high and carried gaily, but not over back or curled. Should be of good strength, anything approaching a "pipe-stopper" tail being especially objectionable.

Legs: Forelegs viewed from any direction must be straight with bone strong right down to feet, showing little or no appearance of ankle in front, and being short and straight in pastern. Both fore and hind legs should be carried straight forward in traveling, stifles not turning outward. Elbows should hang perpendicular to body, working free

of sides. *Feet* should be round, compact, and not large; soles hard and tough; toes moderately arched, and turned neither in nor out.

Coat: Should be smooth, flat, but hard, dense, and abundant. Belly and underside of thighs should not be bare.

Color: White should predominate; brindle, red or liver markings are objectionable. Otherwise this point is of little or no importance.

Symmetry, Size and Character: Dog must present a generally gay, lively, and active appearance; bone and strength in a small compass essential; but this must not be taken to mean that a fox terrier should be cloddy, or in any way coarse—speed and endurance must be looked to as well as power, and the symmetry of the foxhound taken as a model. The terrier, like the hound, must on no account be leggy, nor too short in the leg. He should stand like a cleverly made hunter covering a lot of ground, yet with a short back, as before stated. He will then attain the highest degree of propelling power, together with greatest length of stride compatible with length of body. Weight is not a certain criterion of a terrier's fitness for work—general shape, size, and contour are the main points; if a dog can gallop and stay, and follow his fox up a drain, it matters little what his weight is to a pound or so. According to present-day requirements, a full-sized, well-balanced dog should not exceed 15½ inches (39.4 cm) at the withers—the bitch being proportionately lower—nor should length of back from withers to root of tail exceed 12 inches (30.5 cm) while to maintain relative proportions, head should not exceed 7¼ inches (18.4 cm) or be less than 7 inches (17.8 cm). A dog with these measurements should scale 18 pounds (8.2 kg) in show condition—a bitch weighing some 2 pounds (4.4 kg) less—with a margin of 1 pound (2.2 kg) either way.

Balance: May be defined as the correct proportions of a certain point, or points, when considered

The Bedlington terrier, which is often compared to a lamb (top). An uncombed soft-coated wheaten terrier, believed to be the oldest of the Irish varieties (bottom).

in relation to a certain other point or points. It is the keystone of the terrier's anatomy. Chief points for consideration are relative proportions of skull and foreface; head and back; height at withers and length of body from shoulder-point to buttock—the ideal of proportion being reached when the last two measurements are the same. It should be added that, although head measurements can be taken with absolute accuracy, height at withers and length of back and coat are approximate, and are inserted for the information of breeders and exhibitors rather than as a hard and fast rule.

Movement: Movement, or action, is the crucial test of conformation. The terrier's legs should be carried straight forward while traveling, forelegs hanging perpendicular and swinging parallel with sides, like the pendulum of a clock. The principal propulsive power is furnished by hind legs, perfection of action being found in the terrier possessing long thighs and muscular second thighs well bent at stifles, which admit of a strong forward thrust or "snatch" of hocks. When approaching, forelegs should form a continuation of the straight line of the front, feet being the same distance apart as elbows. When stationary it is often difficult to determine whether a dog is slightly out at shoulder, but, directly he moves, the defect—if it exists— becomes more apparent, forefeet having a tendency to cross, "weave," or "dish." When, on the contrary, the dog is tied at the shoulder, tendency of feet is to move wider apart, with a sort of paddling action. When hocks are turned in—cow-hocks—stifles and feet are turned outwards, resulting in serious loss of propulsive power. When hocks are turned outwards the tendency of hind feet is to cross, resulting in an ungainly waddle.

Official Standard for the Wire Fox Terrier

Characteristics: The terrier should be alert, quick of movement, keen of expression, on the tip-toe of expectation at the slightest provocation. Character is imparted by the expression of the eyes and by the carriage of ears and tail.

General Appearance: The dog should be balanced and this may be defined as the correct proportions of a certain point or points, when considered in relation to a certain other point or points. It is the keystone of the terrier's anatomy. Chief points for consideration are the relative proportions of skull and foreface; head and back; height at withers; and length of body from shoulder-point to buttock—the ideal of proportion being reached when the last two measurements are the same. It should be added that, although the head measurements can be taken with absolute accuracy, the height at withers and length of back are approximate, and are inserted for the information of breeders and exhibitors rather than as a hard-and-fast rule. The movement or action is the crucial test of conformation. The terrier's legs should be carried straight forward while traveling, forelegs hanging perpendicular and swinging parallel to sides, like the pendulum of a clock. Principal propulsive power is furnished by hind legs, perfection of action being found in the terrier possessing long thighs and muscular second-thighs well bent at stifles, which admit of a strong forward thrust or "snatch" of hocks. When approaching, forelegs should form a continuation of the straight of the front, feet being the same distance apart as elbows. When stationary it is often difficult to determine whether a dog is slightly out at shoulder but when he moves the defect—if it exists— becomes more apparent, the forefeet having a tendency to cross "weave" or "dish." When, on the contrary, the dog is tied at the shoulder, tendency of feet is to move wider apart, with a sort of paddling action. When hocks are turned in—cowhocks—stifles and feet are turned outwards, resulting in serious loss of propulsive power. When hocks are turned outwards the tendency of hind feet is to cross, resulting in an ungainly waddle.

Head and Skull: Top line of skull should be almost flat, sloping slightly and gradually decreasing in width towards eyes, and should not exceed 3½ inches (8.9 cm) in diameter at widest part—measuirng with calipers—in the full-grown dog of correct size; bitch's skull being proportionately narrower. If this measurement is exceeded, skull is termed "coarse," while a full-grown dog with a much narrower skull is termed "bitchy" in head. Length of head of a full-grown well-developed dog of correct size—measured with calipers—from back of occipital bone to nostrils—should be from 7–7¼ inches (17.9–18.5 cm), the bitch's head being proportionately shorter. Any measurement in excess of this usually indicates an oversized or long-backed specimen, although occasionally—so rarely as to partake of the nature of a freak—a terrier of correct size may boast a head 7½ inches (19.2 cm) in length. In a well-balanced head there should be little apparent difference in length between skull and foreface. If, however, foreface is noticeably shorter, it amounts to a fault, head looking weak and "unfinished." On the other hand, when eyes are set too high up in skull and too near ears, it also amounts to a fault, head being said to have a "foreign appearance." Although foreface should gradually taper from eye to muzzle and should dip slightly at its juncture with forehead, it should not "dish" or fall away quickly below eyes, where it should be full and well made up, but relieved from "wedginess" by a little delicate chiseling. While well-developed jawbones, armed with set of strong, white teeth, impart that appearance of strength to foreface which is so desirable, an excessive bony or muscular development of jaws is both unnecessary and unsightly, as it is partly responsible for the full and rounded contour of cheeks to which the term "cheeky" is applied. Nose should be black. *Eyes:* Should be dark, moderately small, rather deep-set, not prominent, and full of fire, life, and intelligence; as nearly as possible circular, and not too far apart. Anything approaching a yellow eye is most objectionable. *Ears:* Should be small and V-shaped and of moderate thickness, flaps neatly folded over and drooping forward close to cheeks. Top line of folded ear should be well above level of skull. A pendulous ear, hanging dead by side of head like a hound's, is uncharacteristic of the terrier, while an ear which is semierect is still more undesirable. *Mouth:* Both upper and lower jaws should be strong and muscular, teeth nearly as possible level and capable of closing together like a vise—lower canines locking in front of upper and points of upper incisors slightly overlapping lower.

Neck: Should be clean, muscular, of fair length, free from throatiness, and presenting a graceful curve when viewed from side.

Forequarters: Shoulders when viewed from front should slope steeply downwards from their juncture, with neck towards points, which should be fine. When viewed from side they should be long, well laid back, and should slope obliquely backwards from points to withers, which should always be clean cut. A shoulder well laid back gives the long forehand which, in combination with short back, is so desirable in terrier or hunter. Chest deep and not broad, a too narrow chest almost as undesirable as a very broad one. Excessive depth of chest and brisket is an impediment to a terrier when going to ground. Viewed from any direction legs should be straight, bone of forelegs strong right down to feet. Elbows should hang perpendicular to body, working free of sides, carried straight through in traveling.

Description of Terrier Breeds

Body: Back should be short and level with no appearance of slackness—loins muscular and very slightly arched. Brisket should be deep, front ribs moderately arched; back ribs deep and well sprung. The term "slackness" is applied both to portion of back immediately behind withers when it shows any tendency to dip, and also flanks when there is too much space between back ribs and hipbone. When there is little space between ribs and hips, dog is said to be "short in couplings," "short-coupled," or "well-ribbed up." A terrier can scarcely be too short in back, provided he has sufficient length of neck and liberty of movement. The bitch may be slightly longer in couplings than the dog.

Hindquarters: Should be strong and muscular, quite free from droop or crouch; thighs long and powerful; stifles well curved and turned neither in nor out; hock joints well bent and near the ground; hocks perfectly upright and parallel with each other when viewed from behind. Worst possible form of hindquarters consists of short second-thigh and straight stifle, a combination which causes hind legs to act as props rather than instruments of propulsion. Hind legs should be carried straight through in traveling.

Feet: Should be round, compact, and not large—pads tough and well cushioned; toes moderately arched and turned neither in nor out. A terrier with good-shaped forelegs and feet will wear his nails down short by contact with road surface, weight of body being evenly distributed between toe pads and heels.

Tail: Should be set on rather high and carried gaily but not curled. Should be of good strength and substance and of fair length—a three-quarters dock is about right—since it affords the only safe grip when handling working terriers. Very short tail suitable neither for work nor show.

Coat: Best coats appear to be broken, hairs having a tendency to twist, and are of dense, wiry texture—like coconut matting—hairs growing so closely and strongly together that when parted with the fingers skin cannot be seen. At the base of these stiff hairs is a shorter growth of finer and softer hair—termed the undercoat. Coat on sides is never quite so hard as that on back and quarters. Some of the hardest coats are "crinkly" or slightly waved, but a curly coat is very objectionable. Hair on upper and lower jaws should be crisp and only sufficiently long to impart an appearance of strength to foreface. Hair on forelegs should also be dense and crisp. Coat should average in length from $^3/_4$ to 1 inch (1.9–2.5 cm) on shoulders and neck, lengthening to $1^1/_2$ inches (3.8 cm) on withers, backs, ribs, and quarters. These measurements are given rather as a guide to exhibitors than as an infallible rule, since length of coat depends on climate, seasons, and individual animal. Judge must form own opinion as to what constitutes a "sufficient" coat on the day.

Color: White should predominate; brindle, red, liver, or slaty blue are objectionable. Otherwise, color is of little or no importance.

Weight and Size: Bone and strength in a small compass are essential, but this must not be taken to mean that a terrier should be "cloddy," or in any way coarse—speed and endurance requisite as well as power. The terrier must on no account be leggy, nor too short on the leg. He should stand like a cleverly-made, short-backed hunter, covering a lot of ground. According to present-day requirements, a full-sized, well-balanced dog should not exceed $15^1/_2$ inches (39.4 cm) at the withers—the bitch being proportionately lower—nor should the length of back from withers to root of tail exceed 12 inches (30.5 cm) while to maintain the relative proportions, head—as before mentioned—should not exceed $7^1/_4$ inches (18.4 cm) or be less than 7 inches (17.8 cm). A dog with these measurements should scale 18 pounds (8.2 kg) in show condition—a bitch weighing some 2 pounds (0.9 kg) less—with a margin of 1 pound (0.45 kg) either way.

Irish Terrier

This breed dates back several centuries to the homes of Irish laborers, who used their dogs to rid the fields of small predators. The Irish terrier proved itself an all-around worker, eagerly turning to any task its master required of it—whether guarding the home, flushing a fox, or being a sporting companion.

Irish terriers, puppy and adult.

This dog typifies the legendary terrier courage, but intense gameness is easily tempered by early training and the result is a superb house pet. It will thrive in any environment, in any size home, but requires some additional daily exercise beyond what is gained in the normal course of an active terrier's day. The Irish terrier is not much for relaxation, and prefers to keep itself busy by investigating its surroundings for any new object of interest. It takes eagerly to the attention of children and can be trusted to be sensible in its reaction to unintentional rough treatment.

The Irish terrier is moderately sized, averaging 18 inches (46.0 cm) in height and weighing 25 to 27 pounds (11.3–12.2 kg). It has a long, narrow head with small, V-shaped ears and expressive eyes. The coat is dense and wiry and requires only routine brushing and combing. It varies in color from bright red to wheaten, and any scraggly hairs are easily removed by plucking.

Loyal to the extreme, the Irish terrier is a natural watchdog. It is quick to investigate all unusual noises and inspects all visitors to the household. If the need should arise, this dog would immediately come to the defense of its masters. This instinct for the fight will also quickly surface when male meets male, so care should be taken if more than one dog is to be kept in the home.

The Irish terrier is a hardy dog with few health or whelping problems. Litters generally contain four to seven puppies. The young may have a darker coat due to some black hairs that will disappear as the dogs mature.

Official Standard for the Irish Terrier

Head: Long, but in nice proportion to rest of body; skull flat, rather narrow between ears, and narrowing slightly toward eyes; free from wrinkle, with stop hardly noticeable except in profile. Jaws must be strong and muscular, but not too full in cheek, and of good punishing length. Foreface must not fall away appreciably between or below eyes; instead, modeling should be delicate. Exaggerated foreface, or noticeably short foreface, disturbs proper balance of head and is not desirable. Foreface and skull from occiput to stop should be approximately equal in length. Excessive muscular development of cheeks, or bony development of temples, conditions which are described by the fancier as "cheeky," or "strong in head," or "thick in skull" are objectionable. "Bumpy" head, in which skull presents two lumps of bony structure above eyes, is to be faulted. Hair on upper and lower jaws should be similar in quality and texture to that on body, and of sufficient length to

Description of Terrier Breeds

present an appearance of additional strength and finish to foreface. Either profuse, goatlike beard, or absence of beard, is unsightly and undesirable. *Teeth:* Should be strong and even, white and sound; and neither overshot nor undershot. *Lips:* Should be close and well-fitting, almost black in color. *Nose:* Must be black. *Eyes:* Dark brown; small, not prominent; full of life, fire, and intelligence, showing an intense expression. The light or yellow eye is most objectionable, and is a bad fault. *Ears:* Small and V-shaped; of moderate thickness; set well on head, and dropping forward closely toward outside corner of eye. Top of folded ear should be well above level of skull. A "dead" ear, houndlike in appearance, must be severely penalized. It is not characteristic of the Irish terrier. Hair should be much shorter and somewhat darker than that on body.

Neck: Should be of fair length and gradually widening toward shoulders; well and proudly carried, and free from throatiness. Generally there is a slight frill in hair at each side of neck, extending almost to corner of ear.

Shoulders and Chest: Must be fine, long, and sloping well into back. Chest should be deep and muscular, but neither full nor wide.

Body: Should be moderately long. Short back is not characteristic of the Irish terrier, and is extremely objectionable. Back must be strong and straight, and free from appearance of slackness or "dip" behind shoulders. Loin should be strong and muscular, and slightly arched, ribs fairly sprung, deep rather than round, reaching to level of elbow. Bitch may be slightly longer than the dog.

Hindquarters: Should be strong and muscular; thighs powerful; hocks near the ground; stifles moderately bent.

Stern: Should be docked, taking off about one quarter. Should be set on rather high, but not curled. Should be of good strength and substance; of fair length and well covered with harsh, rough hair.

Feet and Legs: Feet should be strong, tolerably round, and moderately small; toes arched and turned neither out nor in, with dark toenails. Pads should be deep, and must be perfectly sound and free from corns. Cracks alone do not necessarily indicate unsound feet. In fact, all breeds have cracked pads occasionally, from various causes. Legs moderately long, well set from shoulders, perfectly straight, with plenty of bone and muscle; elbows working clear of sides; pasterns short, straight, and hardly noticeable. Both fore and hind legs should move straight forward when traveling; stifles should not turn outwards. "Cowhocks"—that is, the hocks turned in and the feet turned out—are intolerable. Legs should be free from feather and covered with hair of similar texture to that on body to give proper finish to the dog.

Coat: Should be dense and wiry in texture, rich in quality, having a broken appearance, but still lying fairly close to body, hairs growing so closely and strongly together that when parted with the fingers skin is hardly visible; free of softness or silkiness, and not so long as to alter outline of body, particularly in hindquarters. On sides of body the coat is never as harsh as on back and quarters, but it should be plentiful and of good texture. At base of stiff outer coat there should be a growth of finer and softer hair, lighter in color, termed the undercoat. Single coats, without any undercoat, and wavy coats are undesirable; curly and kinky coats are most objectionable.

Color: Should be whole-colored; bright red, golden red, red wheaten, or wheaten. Small patch of white on chest, frequently encountered in all whole-colored breeds, is permissible but not desirable. White on any other part of body is most objectionable. Puppies sometimes have black hair at birth, which should disappear before they are full grown.

Size: Most desirable weight in show condition is 27 pounds (12.2 kg) for the dog and 25 pounds

(11.3 kg) for the bitch. Height at shoulder should be approximately 18 inches (46.0 cm). These figures serve as a guide to both breeder and judge. In the show ring, however, the informed judge readily identifies the oversized or undersized Irish terrier by its conformation and general appearance. Weight is not the last word in judgment. It is of greatest importance to select, insofar as possible, terriers of moderate and generally accepted size, possessing the other various characteristics.

General Appearance: Overall appearance of the Irish terrier is important. In conformation he must be more than a sum of his parts. He must be all-of-a-piece, a balanced vital picture of symmetry, proportion, and harmony. Furthermore, he must convey character. This terrier must be active, lithe, and wiry in movement, with great animation; sturdy and strong in substance and bone structure, but at the same time free from clumsiness, for speed, power, and endurance are most essential. The Irish terrier must be neither "cobby" nor "cloddy," but should be built on lines of speed with a graceful, racing outline.

Temperament: Temperament of the Irish terrier reflects his early background: he was family pet, guard dog, and hunter. He is good-tempered, spirited and game. It is of the utmost importance that the Irish terrier show fire and animation. There is a heedless, reckless pluck about the Irish terrier which is characteristic, and which, coupled with the headlong dash, blind to all consequences, with which he rushes at his adversary, has earned for the breed the proud epithet of "Daredevil." He is of good temper, most affectionate, and absolutely loyal to mankind. Tender and forebearing with those he loves, this rugged, stouthearted terrier will guard his master, his mistress, and children with utter contempt for danger or hurt. His life is one continuous and eager offering of loyal and faithful companionship and devotion. He is ever on guard, and stands between his home and all that threatens.

Kerry Blue Terrier

This lighthearted breed takes its name from the County Kerry area of Ireland, where this terrier has long been used as a working, hunting, and companion dog. It dates back to the 1800s and was owned primarily by County Kerry farmers, who valued the breed's feisty temperament and mischievous nature.

It is one of the larger terriers, averaging around 18 to 19 inches (46.0–48.2 cm) at the withers and up to 40 pounds (18.1 kg) in weight. It is muscular and well balanced, with small, V-shaped ears and an erectly carried docked tail. It is every bit the terrier, from its solid conformation and angular profile to its spunky personality.

Kerry blue terriers, puppy and adult.

The Kerry blue's distinctive blue-gray coat is the hallmark of the breed. It is a soft, dense coat that sheds very little and seldom gives off an offensive odor. There is no downy undercoat that is typically found in most terrier breeds. The coat is not without grooming requirements, however. It must be regularly and thoroughly brushed and combed (daily is best), and needs clipping every few months. The necessary trimming can be mastered with proper instruction and lots of practice; however, some owners may prefer to leave this task to a professional groomer.

This breed is generally very robust and can be long-lived. There is a slight tendency toward eye problems. Kerry blue litters generally contain five to eight puppies, and they will appear nearly black at birth. It takes 18 months or more for the final coat color to stabilize.

The Kerry blue is very personable and enjoys the company of humans more than that of other dogs. It can be an aggressive breed and it will never back down from a challenge or a fight with another dog; this is particularly prevalent when male meets male. The owner of a Kerry blue terrier must be a firm disciplinarian, as this breed is extremely determined and strong-willed. Obedience training is a must; be prepared for some confrontations during the early lessons. Once the dog accepts a master, however, it can learn quickly and efficiently. Kerry blues have done very well in obedience competition.

While the Kerry blue does not require extensive exercise, it is recommended that the dog be allowed a spirited run at regular intervals. The breed does best in a home with a yard, rather than in an apartment. It is a natural watchdog and will devotedly protect its loved ones. The Kerry blue is at its best when surrounded by people and will often create little games to amuse those around it. It is jovial, fun-loving, and above all enthusiastic.

Official Standard for the Kerry Blue Terrier

Head: Long, but not exaggerated, in good proportion to rest of body. Well-balanced, with little apparent difference between length of skull and foreface. *Skull:* Flat, with very slight stop, of but moderate breadth between ears, and narrowing very slightly to eyes. *Cheeks:* Clean and level, free from bumpiness. *Ears:* V-shaped, small but not out of proportion to size of dog, of moderate thickness, carried forward close to cheeks with top of folded ear slightly above level of skull. A "dead" ear, houndlike in appearance, is very undesirable. *Foreface:* Jaws deep, strong, and muscular. Foreface full and well made up, not falling away appreciably below eyes but moderately chiseled out to relieve foreface from wedginess. *Nose:* Black, nostrils large and wide. *Teeth:* Strong, white, and either level or with upper (incisor) teeth slightly overlapping lower teeth. An undershot mouth should be strictly penalized. *Eyes:* Dark, small, not prominent, well placed, and with a keen terrier expression. Anything approaching a yellow eye is very undesirable.

Neck: Clean and moderately long, gradually widening to shoulders upon which it should be well set and carried proudly.

Shoulders and Chest: Shoulders fine, long and sloping, well laid back and well knit. Chest deep and of but moderate breadth.

Legs and Feet: Legs moderately long with plenty of bone and muscle. Forelegs should be straight from both front and side view, with elbows hanging perpendicularly to body and working clear of sides in movement, pasterns short, straight and hardly noticeable. Both forelegs and hind legs should move straight forward when traveling, stifles turning neither in nor out. *Feet* should be strong, compact, fairly round, and moderately small, with good depth of pad free from cracks, toes arched, turned neither in nor out, with black toenails.

Body: Back short, strong and straight (*i.e.* level), with no appearance of slackness. Loin short and powerful with a slight tuck-up, ribs fairly well sprung, deep rather than round.

Hindquarters and Stern: Hindquarters strong and muscular with full freedom of action, free from droop or crouch, thighs long and powerful, stifles well bent and turned neither in nor out, hocks near the ground and, when viewed from behind, upright and parallel with each other, the dog standing well up on them. Tail should be set on high, of moderate length, and carried gaily erect, the straighter the tail the better.

Color: Correct mature color is any shade of blue-gray or gray-blue from deep slate to light blue gray, of a fairly uniform color throughout except that distinctly darker to black parts may appear on muzzle, head, ears, tail, and feet. Kerry color, in its process of "clearing" from an apparent black at birth to mature gray-blue or blue-gray, passes through one or more transitions—involving a very dark blue (darker than deep slate), shades or tinges of brown, and mixtures of these, together with a progressive infiltration of the correct mature color. Up to 18 months such deviations from correct mature color are permissible without preference and without regard for uniformity. Thereafter, deviation from it to any significant extent must be severely penalized. Solid black is never permissible in the show ring. Up to 18 months any doubt as to whether a dog is black or a very dark blue should be resolved in favor of the dog, particularly in the case of a puppy. Black on muzzle, head, ears, tail, and feet is permissible at any age.

Coat: Soft, dense, and wavy. Harsh, wire, or bristle coat should be severely penalized. In show trim body should be well covered but tidy, with head (except for whiskers) and ears and cheeks clear.

General Conformation and Character: The typical Kerry blue terrier should be upstanding, well knit and in good balance, showing a well-developed and muscular body with definite terrier style and character throughout. A low-slung Kerry is not typical.

Height: The ideal Kerry should be 18½ inches (47.1 cm) at withers for a dog, slightly less for a bitch. In judging Kerries, a height of 18 to 19½ inches (46.0–50.0 cm) for a dog, and 17½ to 19 inches (44.5–48.3 cm) for a bitch should be given primary preference. Only where the comparative superiority of a specimen outside of the ranges noted clearly justifies it, should greater latitude be taken. In no case should it extend to a dog over 20 inches (51.0 cm) or under 17½ inches (44.5 cm) or to a bitch over 19½ inches (50.0 cm) or under 17 inches (43.2 cm). The minimum limits do not apply to puppies.

Weight: Most desirable weight for a fully developed dog is from 33 to 40 pounds (15–18.1 kg), bitches weighing proportionately less.

Lakeland Terrier

The Lakeland terrier originated in the mountainous northwestern section of England from matings of the native terrier strains with what are thought to be the early Dandie Dinmont and border terrier specimens. The breed was used primarily to keep the area clear of the foxes that preyed on the livestock. This was a dangerous task that required unmatched courage and stamina in a dog with a small, compact body that could squeeze into the foxes' burrows. Lakelands, generally used with teams of hounds during the hunt,

Lakeland terriers, puppies and adult.

were called on to flush the foxes once they went underground. The breed excelled at its work and would willingly dig into a predator's lair to accomplish the assigned task. .

The Lakeland terrier is not found in great numbers in the United States, but this is not a consequence of its personality. It is very personable and enjoys the company of both adults and children. It is a natural watchdog, and is quick to give voice if any noise or movement seems out of place. Like all terriers, the Lakeland is a game, highly energetic breed; this should always be considered by potential owners. It enjoys an active life, and does not take well to the presence of other animals; this is especially true of males.

The dog stands 14 to 15 inches (36.0–38.1 cm) in height and weighs approximately 17 pounds (7.7 kg). It has a rectangular head, small, V-shaped ears, and an intense expression that reveals the dog's self-confidence.

The coat of the Lakeland terrier is two-ply, with a hard outer coat and a soft undercoat. It requires regular brushing and trimming. To maintain the desired texture, you will need to strip or pluck the outer coat. Nonshow dogs can have the coat clipped to an easily manageable length.

The Lakeland is usually very robust, exhibiting no predominant health problems. It requires more exercise than one would suspect for a dog of this size. Litters usually contain from three to six puppies, and a puppy's coat will not reach the proper texture and color until maturity.

Official Standard for the Lakeland Terrier

General Appearance: The Lakeland terrier is a small, workmanlike dog of square, sturdy build and gay, friendly, self-confident demeanor. He stands on his toes as if ready to go, and he moves, lithe and graceful, with a straight-ahead, free stride of good length. His head is rectangular in contour, ears V-shaped, and wiry coat finished off with fairly long furnishings on muzzle and legs.

Head: Well balanced, rectangular, the length of skull equaling length of muzzle when measured from occiput to stop, and from stop to nosetip. *Skull* is flat on top and moderately broad, cheeks almost straightsided, and stop barely perceptible. *Muzzle* is broad with straight nose bridge and good fill-in beneath eyes. *Nose* is black, except that liver-colored noses shall be permissible on liver-coated dogs. *Jaws* are powerful. *Teeth,* which are comparatively large, may meet in either a level, edge-to-edge bite, or a slightly overlapping scissors bite. Specimens with teeth overshot or undershot are to be disqualified. *Ears* are small, V-shaped, their fold just above top of skull, inner edge close to cheeks, and flap pointed down. *Eyes,* moderately small and somewhat oval, set squarely in skull, fairly wide apart. Their normally dark color may be a warm brown or black. *Expression* depends upon the dog's mood of the moment; although typically alert, it may be intense and determined, or gay and even impish.

Neck: Reachy and of good length; refined but strong; clean at throat, slightly arched, and widening gradually into shoulders. Withers, that point at back of neck where neck and body meet, are noticeably higher than level of back.

Body: In overall length-to-height proportion, the dog is approximately square. Moderately narrow *chest* is deep; it extends to elbows which are held close to body. Shoulder blades are sloping, that is, well laid back, their musculature lean and almost flat in outline. *Ribs* are well sprung and moderately rounded. *Back* is short and level in topline. *Loins* are taut and short, although they may be a trifle longer in bitches than in dogs. *Quarters* are strong, broad, and muscular.

Legs and Feet: *Forelegs* are strongly boned, clean, and absolutely straight as viewed from front or side, and devoid of appreciable bend at pasterns. *Hind legs* too are strong and sturdy,

Description of Terrier Breeds

second thighs long and nicely angulated at stifles and hocks. *Hocks* are well let down, with bone from hock to toes straight and parallel to each other. Small *feet* are round, toes compact and well padded, nails strong. Dewclaws, if any, are to be removed.

Tail: Set high on body; customarily docked so that when dog is set up in show position, tip of docked tail is on an approximate level with skull. In carriage it is gay or upright, although a slight curve in direction of head is considered desirable. Tail curled over the back is faulty.

Coat and Color: Two-ply or double, outer coat is hard and wiry in texture, undercoat soft. Furnishings on muzzle and legs are plentiful as opposed to profuse. *Color* may be blue, black, liver, black and tan, blue and tan, red, red grizzle, grizzle and tan, or wheaten. Tan as desirable in the Lakeland terrier, is a light wheaten or straw color, with rich red or mahogany tan to be penalized. Otherwise, colors, as specified, are equally acceptable. Dark-saddled specimens (whether black grizzle or blue) are nearly solid black at birth, with tan points on muzzle and feet. The black recedes and usually turns grayish or grizzle at maturity, while the tan also lightens.

Size: Ideal *height* of mature dog is 14½ inches (37.0 cm) from withers to ground, with up to a ½-inch (1.2 cm) deviation either way permissible. Bitches may measure as much as one inch (2.5 cm) less than dogs. *Weight* of well-balanced, mature specimen in hard show condition, averages approximately 17 pounds (7.7 kg), those of other heights proportionately more or less. Size is to be considered of lesser importance than other qualities, that is, when judging dogs of equal merit, the one nearest the ideal size is to be preferred. Symmetry and proportion, however, are paramount in the appraisal, since all qualities together must be considered in visualizing the ideal.

Movement: Straight and free, with good length of stride. Paddling, moving close, and toeing-in are faulty.

Temperament: The typical Lakeland terrier is bold, gay, and friendly, with a self-confident, cock-of-the-walk attitude. Shyness, especially shy-sharpness, in the mature specimen is to be heavily penalized.

Manchester Terrier (Standard and Toy)

The Manchester terrier is one of the oldest terrier breeds, tracing its ancestry back as far as the 1500s. These dogs were highly valued for their usefulness as rat catchers; pound for pound they had no match when it came to courage and native smartness. Over the years crosses to sighthounds, probably whippets, helped rid the breed of its coarseness and to give it extra speed for hunting rabbits. The breed was originally known as the black-and-tan terrier, but it flourished in the Manchester section of England and was officially given this town's name in the 1920s.

Manchester terriers, standard and toy.

Description of Terrier Breeds

This breed is found in two sizes. The standard variety Manchester terrier weighs from 12 to 22 pounds (5.4–10 kg), while the toy variety (which is placed in the toy group) weighs less than 12 pounds (5.4 kg). Many toy Manchesters are 5 pounds and less. Maximum and minimum heights are not listed in the breed standard, but standard variety Manchesters are generally 15 to 16 inches (38.1–41.0 cm) tall, while the toys are 11 inches or smaller.

The Manchester terrier's coat is jet black with mahogany markings. It is smooth, dense, and exceptionally glossy. Grooming requirements are minimal. An occasional brushing with a bristle brush is enough to keep the coat in fine shape. It is a very hardy breed with few notable health problems. Litters generally range from two to four puppies. Many owners choose to have the puppies' ears cropped. This procedure can be performed when the puppies are eight to ten weeks old, but should be undertaken only by a qualified veterinarian.

In the home the Manchester terrier is a fine pet for all ages. Care should be taken, however, to teach children how to play with the toy variety; with such limited size come restrictions on roughhousing. The Manchester is naturally clean, intelligent, and well-behaved, and will adapt to any surroundings. The Manchester terrier enjoys exercise and frequent walks with its owners and makes its pleasure known by being a very affectionate companion. It is particularly attuned to what is going on around it and sensitive to its loved ones' feelings and moods. While the Manchester terrier is one of the least outwardly aggressive terrier breeds, it still does best when the sole dog in the house.

Official Standard for the Manchester and Toy Manchester Terrier

Head: Long, narrow, tight-skinned, almost flat, with slight indentation up the forehead; slightly wedge-shaped, tapering to nose, with no visible cheek muscles, and well filled up under eyes; tight-lipped jaws, level in mouth, and functionally level teeth, or incisors of upper jaw may make a close, slightly overlapping contact with incisors of the lower jaw. *Eyes:* Small, bright, sparkling and as near black as possible; set moderately close together; olblong in shape, slanting upwards on the outside; should neither protrude nor sink in skull. *Nose:* Black. *Ears (toy variety):* Of moderate size; set well up on skull and rather close together; thin, moderately narrow at base; with pointed tips; naturally erect carriage. Wide, flaring, blunt-tipped or "bell" ears are a serious fault; cropped or cut ears shall disqualify. *Ears (standard variety):* Erect, or button, small and thin; smaller at root and set as close together as possible at top of head. If cropped, to a point, long and carried erect.

Neck and Shoulders: Neck should be moderate length, slim and graceful; gradually becoming larger as it approaches and blends smoothly with sloping shoulders; free from throatiness; slightly arched from occiput.

Chest: Narrow between legs; deep in brisket.

Body: Moderately short, with robust loins; ribs well sprung out behind shoulders; back slightly arched at loin, and falling again to tail to the same height as shoulder.

Legs: Forelegs straight, of proportionate length, and well under body. Hind legs should not turn in or out as viewed from rear; carried back; hocks well let down. *Feet:* Compact, well arched, with jet black nails; two middle toes in front feet rather longer than the others; hind feet shaped like those of a cat.

Description of Terrier Breeds

Tail: Moderately short, and set on where arch of back ends; thick where it joins body, tapering to a point, not carried higher than back.

Coat: Smooth, short, thick, dense, close and glossy; not soft.

Color: Jet black and rich mahogany tan, which should not run or blend into each other but abruptly forming clear, well-defined lines of color division. A small tan spot over each eye; a very small tan spot on each cheek; the lips of upper and lower jaws should be tanned, extending under throat, ending in shape of letter V; inside of ears partly tanned. Tan spots, called "rosettes," on each side of chest above front legs, more pronounced in puppies than in adults. There should be a black "thumb mark" patch on front of each foreleg between pastern and knee. There should be a distinct black "pencil mark" line running lengthwise on top of each toe on all four feet. Remainder of forelegs to be tan to knee. Tan on hind legs should continue from penciling on feet up inside of legs to a little below stifle joint; outside of hind legs to be black. There should be tan under tail, and on vent, but only of such size as to be covered by tail. Any color other than black and tan shall disqualify except that white in any part of coat is a serious fault, and shall disqualify whenever white shall form a patch or stripe measuring as much as $\frac{1}{2}$-inch (1.2 cm) in its longest dimension.

Weight *(toy variety):* Not exceeding 12 pounds (5.4 kg). It is suggested that clubs consider dividing the American-bred and open classes by weight as follows: 7 pounds (3.2 kg) and under, over 7 pounds (3.2 kg) and not exceeding 12 pounds (5.4 kg).

Weight *(standard variety):* Over 12 pounds (5.4 kg) and not exceeding 22 pounds (10 kg). Dogs weighing over 22 pounds (10 kg) shall be disqualified. It is suggested that clubs consider dividing the American-bred and open classes by weight as follows: over 12 pounds (5.4 kg) and not exceeding 16 pounds (7.3 kg), over 16 pounds (7.3 kg) and not exceeding 22 pounds (10 kg).

Norfolk and Norwich Terriers

While the Norfolk and Norwich terriers stand only 10 inches (25.4 cm) in height and weigh a mere 11 to 12 pounds (5.0–5.4 kg), they are every ounce the terrier. These breeds date from the early 1800s in the Norwich section of England. The Norwich, and its sister breed the Norfolk, were fostered by the country farmers to help clear the fields of small predators. These terriers were valued for their courage, stamina, and ease of care. Their harsh double coat was weather-resistant and trouble-free, and these dogs proved themselves tireless workers, willing to dig into any furrow in search of game. This trait also led to their popularity as a hunting companion for the gentry, who would use them to flush the fox that went underground during the hunt. The tail of the Norfolk and Norwich has traditionally been docked to a medium length so that it could be grasped to help extricate the dog, if, in its feisty determination, it dug itself in too deeply during a chase.

Norfolk terrier (left), Norwich terrier (right).

Description of Terrier Breeds

For many years the Norfolk and Norwich terriers were regarded as two varieties within the same breed, differentiated by their ear set. In 1979 the breeds were separated by the American Kennel Club, following the action taken in England by the United Kennel Club in 1964. The Norfolk has small, dropped ears, while the Norwich has medium-sized, erect ears.

Today's Norfolk and Norwich terriers are ideal companions for all. Their exercise requirements are moderate, yet they can participate in the most vigorous of activities. Always bear in mind that these breeds were originally working terriers and still exhibit many of the traits that served the early specimens of the breed so well. The most troublesome trait is the desire to dig. These little terriers can do quite a bit of damage to a garden—especially if they spot a rabbit running for cover. The Norfolk and Norwich can also be escape artists, so set fences deeply to prevent these dogs from digging their way to freedom. Another inborn tendency is to chase after all small animals, so keep these dogs on leash whenever not in a confined location.

The personable Norfolk and Norwich terriers thrive on attention and can get along with young and old. They are trustworthy around children, and intensely loyal. If startled or threatened, they can be relied upon to react with restraint. Such self-control is sometimes lacking in other terrier breeds. They also distinguish themselves from other terriers by living rather peacefully with other household pets. They are natural watchdogs and will maintain a constant eye on the goings on around them, giving ample voice in the event of any strange sound or occurrence.

The Norfolk and Norwich are healthy breeds and often quite long-lived. There are generally no whelping problems, and litters usually contain three or four puppies.

Official Standard for the Norfolk Terrier

General Appearance and Characteristics: The Norfolk terrier, game and hardy, with expressive dropped ears, is one of the smallest of the working terriers. It is active and compact, free-moving, with good substance and bone. With its natural, weather-resistant coat and short legs, it is a "perfect demon" in the field. This versatile, agreeable breed can go to ground, bolt a fox and tackle or dispatch other small vermin, working alone or with a pack. Honorable scars from fair wear and tear are acceptable in the ring.

Head: Skull wide, slight rounded, with good width between ears. Muzzle is strong and wedge shaped. Length one-third less than measurement from occiput to well-defined stop. *Ears:* Neatly dropped, small, with break at skull line, carried close to cheek and not falling lower than outer corner of eye. V-shaped, slightly rounded at tip, smooth and velvety to the touch. *Eyes:* Small, dark and oval, with black rims. Placed well apart with a sparkling, keen and intelligent expression. *Mouth:* Jaw clean and strong. Tight-lipped with large teeth and scissors bite.

Forequarters: Neck of medium length, strong and blending into well laid back shoulders—good width of chest, elbows close to ribs, pasterns firm. Short, powerful legs, as straight as is consistent with the digging terrier.

Body: Length of back from point of withers to base of tail should be slightly longer than height at withers. Ribs well sprung, chest moderately deep. Strong loins and level topline.

Hindquarters: Broad with strong, muscular thighs. Good turn of stifle. Hocks well let down and straight when viewed from rear.

Feet: Round, pads thick, with strong, black nails.

Tail: Medium docked, of sufficient length to ensure a balanced outline. Straight, set on high, base level with topline. Not a squirrel tail.

Coat: Protective coat is hard, wiry and straight, about 1½ to 2 inches (3.8–5.1 cm) long, lying

Description of Terrier Breeds

close to body, with definite undercoat. Mane on neck and shoulders longer and also forms ruff at base of ears and throat. Moderate furnishings of harsh texture on legs. Hair on head and ears short and smooth, except for slight eyebrows and whiskers. Some tidying necessary to keep dog neat, but shaping should be heavily penalized.

Color: All shades of red, wheaten, black and tan, or grizzle. Dark points permissible. White marks not desirable.

Gait: Should be true, low, and driving. In front, legs extend forward from shoulder. Good rear angulation showing great powers of propulsion. Viewed from side, hind legs follow in the track of forelegs, moving smoothly from hip and flexing well at stifle and hock. Topline remains level.

Size: Height at withers 9 to 10 inches (23.0–25.4 cm) at maturity. Bitches tend to be smaller than dogs. Weight 11 to 12 pounds (5.0–5.4 kg) or that which is suitable for each individual dog's structure and balance. Fit working condition is a prime consideration.

Temperament: Alert, gregarious, fearless, and loyal. Never aggressive.

Official Standard for the Norwich Terrier

General Appearance and Characteristics: The Norwich terrier, spirited and stocky with sensitive prick ears and a slightly foxy expression, is one of the smallest working terriers. This sturdy descendant of ratting companions, eager to dispatch small vermin alone or in a pack, has good bone and substance and an almost weatherproof coat. A hardy hunt terrier—honorable scars from fair wear and tear are acceptable. Adaptable and sporting, they make ideal companions.

Head: Skull broad and slightly rounded with good width between ears. Muzzle wedge-shaped and strong. Length is about one-third less than the measurement from occiput to well-defined stop. *Ears:* Medium size and erect. Set well apart with pointed tips. Upright when alert.

Eyes: Small, dark, and oval-shaped, with black rims. Placed well apart with a bright and keen expression. *Mouth:* scissors bite. Jaw is clean, strong, and tight-lipped with large teeth. Nose and lip pigment black.

Forequarters: Neck medium length, strong and blending into well laid back shoulders—good width of chest, elbows close to ribs, pasterns firm. Short, powerful legs, as straight as is consistent with the digging terrier.

Body: Moderately short. Compact and deep with level topline. Well-sprung ribs and short loins. Distance from top of withers to ground and from withers to base of tail approximately equal.

Hindquarters: Broad, strong, and muscular with well-turned stifles. Hocks low set and straight when viewed from rear.

Feet: Round with thick pads. Feet point forward when standing or moving. Nails black.

Tail: Medium docked. The terrier's working origin requires that the tail be of sufficient length to grasp. Base level with topline; carried erect.

Coat: Hard, wiry, and straight, lying close to body with a definite undercoat. Coat on neck and shoulders forms a protective mane. Hair on head, ears, and muzzle, except for slight eyebrows and whiskers, short and smooth. This breed should be shown with as natural a coat as possible. A minimum of tidying permissible but shaping should be heavily penalized.

Color: All shades of red, wheaten, black and tan, or grizzle. White marks not desirable.

Gait: Legs moving parallel, extending forward, showing great powers of propulsion. Good rear angulation with a true, yet driving movement. Forelegs move freely with feet and elbows the same distance apart, converging slightly with increased pace. Hind legs follow in the track of forelegs, flexing well at stifle and hock. Topline remains level.

Size: One of the smallest of the terriers, ideal height should not exceed 10 inches (25.6 cm) at withers. Weight approximately 12 pounds (5.4

107

kg). It should be in proportion to the individual dog's structure and balance. Fit working condition is a prime consideration.

Temperament: Gay, fearless, loyal, and affectionate.

Schnauzer, Miniature

The miniature schnauzer is the most popular breed assigned to the Terrier Group by the American Kennel Club and is, in fact, one of the most popular of all recognized breeds. Unlike most terriers, the miniature schnauzer does not hail from the British Isles. It is German in origin, having descended from the larger standard schnauzer. The theory is that the small size of the miniature schnauzer was arrived at through crossings with Affenpinschers during the formative years of the breed.

Today there are three distinct schnauzer breeds: the standard, miniature, and giant. All three share a working dog heritage, with the miniature especially adept as a ratter and stable dog. The miniature is a courageous dog, but less aggressive and quarrelsome than most terriers, including its larger namesakes. It is also less prone to the high-strung antics regarded as typical of the terriers.

In the home, the miniature schnauzer has proven itself to be outgoing, well-mannered, and personable. It gets along with people of all ages, and is notably long on patience with the antics of children. This breed dislikes extended separations from its master, and would prefer to travel along rather than be left behind. Unlike many terriers, it is tolerant of other animals in the home and rarely involves itself in fights or shows of aggression. Its exercise requirements are not extensive, although regular workouts are advised to keep the dog in optimal physical condition. It thrives in all types of environments and households.

Schnauzers, giant, standard, and miniature.

The miniature schnauzer is one of the most intelligent terriers and has had good success in mastering the rigors of competitive obedience training. As with all headstrong breeds, a basic amount of obedience training is advised even if you have no intention of competing.

In appearance, the miniature schnauzer is a compact, stocky dog standing 12 to 14 inches (31.0–36.0 cm) in height and weighing approximately 15 pounds (6.8 kg). Its distinctive facial look is derived from regular groomings to shape the whiskers and bushy eyebrows that are characteristic of the breed. It sports a double coat, with a hard, wiry outer coat and a close undercoat.

Welsh terrier puppies (top left) and adult (top right). Irish terrier adult (bottom left) and puppies (bottom right).

Description of Terrier Breeds

The typical color is salt and pepper in shades of gray. To retain the correct texture for show competition, the coat must be regularly plucked and stripped. Owners of pet-quality miniatures often prefer to go the easier route and have the coat clipped (usually three or four times a year) to keep the dog looking tidy.

Miniature schnauzers are normally quite healthy and long-lived. There is some tendency toward eye problems and urinary tract disorders. Litters average from three to six puppies, with the offspring born darker than they will appear as adults. The tail is docked quite short, so that it is just visible over the topline of the body when erect. The ears of the miniature pinscher are typically cropped, although there has been a trend in recent years toward uncropped ears.

Official Standard for the Miniature Schnauzer

General Appearance: The miniature schnauzer is a robust, active dog of terrier type, resembling his larger cousin, the standard schnauzer, in general appearance, and of an alert, active disposition. He is sturdily built, nearly square in proportion of body length to height, with plenty of bone, and without any suggestion of toyishness.

Temperament: The typical miniature schnauzer is alert and spirited, yet obedient to command. He is friendly, intelligent, and willing to please. He should never be over-aggressive or timid.

Head: Strong and rectangular, its width diminishing slightly from ears to eyes, and again to tip of nose. Forehead unwrinkled. Topskull flat and fairly long. Foreface parallel to topskull, with a slight stop, and is at least as long as topskull. Muzzle strong in proportion to skull; it ends in a moderately blunt manner, with thick whiskers which accentuate rectangular shape of head. *Teeth:* Meet in a scissors bite, that is, upper front teeth overlap lower front teeth in such a manner that inner surface of upper incisors barely touches outer surface of lower incisors when mouth is closed. *Eyes:* Small, dark brown, and deep-set; oval in appearance and keen in expression. *Ears:* When cropped, ears identical in shape and length, with pointed tips; in balance with head and not exaggerated in length; set high on skull and carried perpendicularly at inner edges, with as little bell as possible along outer edges. When uncropped, ears are small and V-shaped, folded close to skull.

Neck: Strong and well arched, blending into shoulders, and with skin fitting tightly at throat.

Body: Short and deep, with brisket extending at least to elbows. Ribs well sprung and deep, extending well back to a short loin. Underbody does not present a tucked-up appearance at flank. Topline is straight; it declines slightly from withers to base of tail. Overall length from chest to stern bone appears to equal height at withers.

Forequarters: Have flat, somewhat sloping shoulders and high withers. Forelegs straight and parallel when viewed from all sides; strong pasterns and good bone; separated by a fairly deep brisket which precludes a pinched front. Elbows close, and ribs spread gradually from first rib so as to allow space for elbows to move close to body.

Hindquarters: Have strong-muscled, slanting thighs: well bent at stifles and straight from hock to so-called heel; sufficient angulation so that, in stance, hocks extend beyond tail. Hindquarters never appear overbuilt or higher than the shoulders.

Feet: Short and round (cat feet) with thick, black pads. Toes arched and compact.

Movement: The trot is the gait at which move-

The Lakeland terrier, from England's rugged north (top). The Kerry blue, which originated in County Kerry, Ireland (bottom).

ment is judged. When approaching, forelegs, with elbows close to body, move straight forward, neither too close nor too far apart. Going away, hind legs are straight and travel in same planes as forelegs.

Tail: Set high and carried erect. Docked only long enough to be clearly visible over topline of body when dog is in proper length of coat.

Coat: Double, with hard, wiry outer coat and close undercoat. Head, neck, and body coat must be plucked. When in show condition body coat should be of sufficient length to determine texture. Close covering on neck, ears, and skull. Furnishings fairly thick but not silky.

Size: From 12 to 14 inches (31.0–36.0 cm). Ideal size 13¹/₂ inches (34.3 cm).

Color: Recognized colors are salt and pepper, black and silver, and solid black. Typical color is salt and pepper in shades of gray; tan shading is permissible. Salt and pepper mixture fades out to light gray or silver white in eyebrows, whiskers, cheeks, under throat, across chest, under tail, leg furnishings, under body, and inside legs. Light underbody hair not to rise higher on sides of body than front elbows.

Black and silvers follow same pattern as salt and peppers. Entire salt-and-pepper section must be black.

Black the only solid color allowed. Must be a true black with no gray hairs and no brown tinge except where whiskers may have become discolored. Small white spot on chest permitted.

Schnauzer, Standard

This breed hails from Germany and dates to the 16th century. Although it is classified by the AKC as a member of the working group, its original purpose was in the terrier tradition: rat catcher. The standard schnauzer is not quite as game and challenging as many terrier breeds, but it is very inquisitive, energetic, and eager to please. It has proven itself to be both a fit worker, doing such chores as guard work and retrieving, as well as a very loving, loyal companion.

The standard schnauzer is a medium-sized dog with a square build, harsh coat, docked tail, and ears that are often cropped. It is a very hardy breed with few health problems other than a slight tendency toward hip dysplasia. It takes naturally and eagerly to obedience training and competition, which is a good outlet for its abundant energy and an antidote for its stubborn streak.

The standard schnauzer is a good pet for active people who can devote the needed time to the dog's exercise and discipline training. This breed needs a lot of attention and considers itself an integral part of the family. Its sensitivity to sight and sound make it a natural watchdog. If taught adequate self-control, it will usually get along peacefully with other animals and children, but it can be aggressive, especially to other male dogs. It does not take well to confinement or long periods alone, and may exhibit its frustration in destructive ways.

The standard schnauzer has a harsh, wiry outer coat and a soft undercoat that must be brushed regularly and professionally trimmed several times a year to maintain a tidy appearance. Unruly hairs are generally plucked out with the fingers or a stripping comb, and the whiskers about the face are scissored to maintain the proper appearance. The coat should not be shaved or clipped extensively, as this will affect the texture of the outer coat, which provides protection for the skin. Skin exposure often leads to irritations and sensitivities.

A litter of standard schnauzers usually contains from four to eight puppies. Most bitches make excellent, attentive mothers who may become irritated if the litter is given too much human attention in the early days. If the puppies' ears are to be cropped, this procedure can be performed by a knowledgeable veterinarian at around eight to ten weeks of age. The owner will be required to retape and clean the ears during the healing process.

Official Standard for the Standard Schnauzer

General Appearance: The standard schnauzer is a robust, heavy-set dog, sturdily built with good muscle and plenty of bone; square-built in proportion of body-length to height. His nature combines high-spirited temperament with extreme reliability. His rugged build and dense harsh coat are accentuated by the hallmark of the breed, the arched eyebrows, bristly mustache, and luxuriant whiskers.

Head: Strong, rectangular, and elongated; narrowing slightly from ears to eyes and again to tip of nose. Total length of head is about one half the length of back measured from withers to set-on of tail. Head matches sex and substance of the dog. Top line of muzzle is parallel with top line of skull. There is a slight stop which is accentuated by wiry brows. *Skull (Occiput to Stop):* Moderately broad between ears with width of skull not exceeding two thirds the length of skull. Skull must be flat; neither domed nor bumpy; skin unwrinkled. *Cheeks:* Well-developed chewing muscles, but not so much that "cheekiness" disturbs rectangular head form. *Muzzle:* Strong, and both parallel and equal in length to topskull; ends in moderately blunt wedge with wiry whiskers accenting rectangular shape of head. Nose is large, black, and full. Lips should be black, tight, and not overlapping. *Eyes:* Medium size; dark brown; oval and turned forward; neither round nor protruding. Brow is arched and wiry, but vision is not impaired nor eyes hidden by too long an eyebrow. *Bite:* Full complement of white teeth, with strong, sound scissors bite. Canine teeth strong and well developed with upper incisors slightly overlapping and engaging lower. Upper and lower jaws powerful and neither overshot nor undershot. *Ears:* Evenly shaped, set high and carried erect when cropped. If uncropped, they are small, V-shaped button ears of moderate thickness and carried rather high and close to head.

Neck: Strong, of moderate thickness and length, elegantly arched and blending cleanly into shoulders. Skin is tight, fitting closely to dry throat with no wrinkles or dewlaps.

Shoulders: Sloping shoulder blades strongly muscled, yet flat and well laid back so that rounded upper ends are in a nearly vertical line above elbows. Slope well forward to point where they join upper arm, forming as nearly as possible a right angle when seen from side. Such an angulation permits maximum forward extension of forelegs without binding or effort.

Chest: Of medium width with well-sprung ribs, and if it could be seen in cross-section would be oval. The breastbone is plainly discernible. Brisket must descend at least to elbows and ascend gradually to rear with belly moderately drawn up.

Body: Compact, strong, short-coupled and substantial so as to permit great flexibility and agility. Height at the highest point of withers equals length from breastbone to point of rump.

Back: Strong, stiff, straight and short, with a well-developed loin section; distance from last rib to hips as short as possible. Top line of back should not be absolutely horizontal, but should have slightly descending slope from first vertebra of withers to faintly curved croup and set-on of tail.

Forelegs: Straight, vertical, and without any curvature when seen from all sides; set moderately far apart; with heavy bone; elbows set close to body and pointing directly to rear.

Description of Terrier Breeds

Hindquarters: Strongly muscled, in balance with forequarters, never appearing higher than shoulders. Croup full and slightly rounded. Thighs broad with well-bent stifles. Second thigh, from knee to hock, approximately parallel with an extension of upper-neck line. Legs, from clearly defined hock joint to feet, short and perpendicular to ground and when viewed from rear are parallel to each other.

Feet: Small and compact, round with thick pads and strong black nails. Toes are well closed and arched (cat's paws) and pointing straight ahead. *Dewclaws:* If any, on the hind legs are generally removed. Dewclaws on forelegs may be removed.

Tail: Set moderately high and carried erect. Docked to not less than 1 inch (2.5 cm) nor more than 2 inches (5.1 cm).

Height: Ideal height at highest point of shoulder blades, $18^1/_2$ to $19^1/_2$ inches (47.0–50.0 cm) for males and $17^1/_2$ inches to $18^1/_2$ inches (44.5–47.0 cm) for females. Dogs measuring over or under these limits must be faulted in proportion to extent of deviation. Dogs measuring more than $^1/_2$ inch (1.2 cm) over or under these limits must be disqualified.

Coat: Tight, hard, wiry, and as thick as possible, composed of a soft, close undercoat and a harsh outer coat which, when seen against the grain, stands up off the back, lying neither smooth nor flat. The outer coat (body coat) is trimmed (by plucking) only to accent the body outline. When in show condition, the outer coat's proper length is approximately $1^1/_2$ inches (3.8 cm), except on ears, head, neck, chest, belly, and under tail where it may be closely trimmed to give the desired typical appearance of the breed. On muzzle and over eyes the coat lengthens to form luxuriant beard and eyebrows; hair on legs is longer than that on body. These "furnishings" should be of harsh texture and should not be so profuse as to detract from neat appearance or working capabilities of the dog.

Color: Pepper and salt or pure black. *Pepper and Salt:* Typical pepper and salt color of topcoat results from combination of black and white hairs, and white hairs banded with black. Acceptable are all shades of pepper and salt and dark iron-gray to silver-gray. Ideally, pepper and salt standard schnauzers have a gray undercoat, but a tan or fawn undercoat is not to be penalized. It is desirable to have a darker facial mask that harmonizes with the particular shade of coat color. Also, in pepper and salt dogs, pepper and salt mixture may fade out to light gray or silver-white in eyebrows, whiskers, cheeks, under throat, across chest, under tail, leg furnishings, under body, and inside legs. *Black:* Ideally the black standard schnauzer should be a true rich color, free from any fading or discoloration or any admixture of gray or tan hairs. Undercoat should also be solid black. However, increased age or continued exposure to sun may cause a certain amount of fading and burning. Small white smudge on chest not a fault. Loss of color as a result of scars from cuts and bites not a fault.

Gait: Sound, strong, quick, free, true, and level gait with powerful, well-angulated hindquarters that reach out and cover ground. Forelegs reach out in a stride balancing that of hindquarters. At a trot, back remains firm and level, without swaying, rolling, or roaching. When viewed from rear, feet, though they may appear to travel close when trotting, must not cross or strike. Increased speed causes feet to converge toward the center line of gravity.

Description of Terrier Breeds

Schnauzer, Giant

The giant schnauzer is well named—it is a giant among dogs. It ranges from 23 to 27 inches (58.4–68.6 cm) in height and can weigh close to 100 pounds (45.4 kg). It is assigned to the working group by the American Kennel Club, as it was originally bred to work with cattle, but among its ancestors were some terrier strains. The breed originated in Germany, where three schnauzer lines developed.

The standard schnauzer is considered to be the original ancestor of the line, and crosses with Bouvier des Flandres and Great Danes were introduced to enhance size and strength.

The giant schnauzer requires adequate space for movement and vigorous exercise, and does best in a household with a large yard and with owners that have time to devote to the needs of a working dog. It is naturally protective of house and home, and often a bit standoffish with strangers. The giant breed does best in a one-dog family, as it may be threatening to other house pets.

The breed's dense, double coat is wiry to the touch. A daily combing and brushing will generally keep it looking tidy, but stray hairs will need to be plucked out regularly. Attaining the sculptured beard and eyebrows that are characteristic of the breed generally requires a professional's touch.

The giant schnauzer gets along well with children as well as adults, but its play is very enthusiastic and may be a little too rough for small children. The sheer size and strength of the breed makes obedience training a must, as an unruly giant would be intolerable.

Like many of the largest breeds, the giant schnauzer has a tendency toward hip dysplasia. Breeding partners should always be x-rayed and certified clear of the problem before mating. The number of puppies in a litter generally ranges from five to eight. While the natural folded ear is becoming increasingly popular, many owners choose to have the puppies' ears cropped at approximately eight to ten weeks of age. This procedure should be attempted only by a qualified veterinarian, but follow-up care at home will be the responsibility of the owner. The ears will need to be rewrapped and checked for proper healing at regular intervals.

Official Standard for the Giant Schnauzer

General Description: The giant schnauzer should resemble, as nearly as possible, in general appearance, a larger and more powerful version of the standard schnauzer, on the whole a bold and valiant figure of a dog. Robust, strongly built, nearly square in proportion of body length to height at withers, active, sturdy, and well muscled. Temperament which combines spirit and alertness with intelligence and reliability. Composed, watchful, courageous, easily trained, deeply loyal to family, playful, amiable in repose, and a commanding figure when aroused. The sound, reliable temperament, rugged build, and dense weather-resistant wiry coat make for one of the most useful, powerful, and enduring working breeds.

Head: Strong, rectangular in appearance, and elongated; narrowing slightly from ears to eyes, and again from eyes to tip of nose. Total length of head is about one-half the length of back (withers to set-on of tail). Head matches the sex and substance of the dog. Top line of muzzle parallel to top line of skull; there is a slight stop accentuated by eyebrows. *Skull:* (Occiput to Stop). Moderately broad between ears; occiput not too prominent. Top of skull flat; skin unwrinkled. *Cheeks:* Flat, but with well-developed chewing muscles; there is no "cheekiness" to disturb rectangular head appearance (with beard). *Muzzle:* Strong and well filled under eyes; both parallel and equal in length to topskull; ending in a moderately blunt wedge. Nose is large, black, and full. Lips are tight, and not overlapping, black in color. *Bite:* A full complement of sound

Description of Terrier Breeds

white teeth (6/6 incisors, 2/2 canines, 8/8 premolars, 4/6 molars) with a scissors bite. Upper and lower jaws powerful and well formed. *Ears:* When cropped, identical in shape and length with pointed tips. In balance with head and not exaggerated in length. Set high on skull and carried perpendicularly at inner edges with as little bell as possible along other edges. When uncropped, ears are V-shaped button ears of medium length and thickness, set high and carried rather high and close to head. *Eyes:* Medium size, dark brown, deep-set. Oval in appearance and keen in expression with lids fitting tightly. Vision is not impaired nor eyes hidden by too long eyebrows.

Neck: Strong and well arched, of moderate length, blending cleanly into shoulders, and with skin fitting tightly at throat; in harmony with the dog's weight and build.

Body: Compact, substantial, short-coupled, and strong, with great power and agility. Height at highest point of withers equals body length from breastbone to point of rump. Loin section well developed, as short as possible for compact build.

Forequarters: Have flat, somewhat sloping shoulders and high withers. Forelegs straight and vertical when viewed from all sides with strong pasterns and good bone; separated by fairly deep brisket which precludes a pinched front. Elbows set close to body and point directly backwards.

Chest: Medium in width, ribs well sprung but with no tendency toward barrel chest; oval in cross section; deep through brisket. Breastbone is plainly discernible, with strong forechest; brisket descends at least to elbows, and ascends gradually toward rear with belly moderately drawn up. Ribs spread gradually from first rib so as to allow space for elbows to move close to body.

Shoulders: Sloping shoulder blades (scapulae) are strongly muscled, yet flat; well laid back so that from the side rounded upper ends are in a nearly vertical line above elbows. Slope well forward to point where they join upper arm

(humerus), forming as nearly as possible a right angle. Such an angulation permits maximum forward extension of forelegs without binding or effort. Both shoulder blades and upper arm are long, permitting depth of chest at brisket.

Back: Short, straight, strong, and firm.

Tail: Set moderately high and carried high in excitement. Should be docked to second or not more than third joint (approximately 1½ to about 3 inches [3.8–7.6 cm] inches long at maturity).

Hindquarters: Strongly muscled, in balance with forequarters; upper thighs slanting and well bent at stifles, with second thighs (tibiae) approximately parallel to an extension of upper neckline. Legs from hock joint to feet are short, perpendicular to ground while dog is standing naturally, and from the rear parallel to each other. Hindquarters do not appear over-built or higher than shoulders. Croup full and slightly rounded.

Feet: Well arched, compact, and catlike, turning neither in nor out, with thick tough pads and dark nails.

Dewclaws: Dewclaws, if any, on hind legs should be removed; on forelegs, may be removed.

Gait: Trot is the gait at which movement is judged. Free, balanced, and vigorous, with good reach in forequarters and good driving power in hindquarters. Rear and front legs are thrown neither in nor out. When moving at a fast trot, a properly built dog will single-track. Back remains strong, firm, and flat.

Coat: Hard, wiry, very dense; composed of a soft undercoat and a harsh outer coat which, when seen against the grain, stands slightly up off the back, lying neither smooth nor flat. Coarse hair on top of head; harsh beard and eyebrows, the schnauzer hallmark.

Color: Solid black or pepper and salt. *Black:* A truly pure black. A small white spot on breast is permitted; any other markings are disqualifying faults. *Pepper and Salt:* Outer coat of a combination of banded hairs (white with black and black with white) and some black and white hairs, appearing gray from a short distance. *Ideally:* An intensely pigmented medium gray shade with "peppering" evenly distributed throughout the coat, and a gray undercoat. *Acceptable:* All shades of pepper and salt from dark iron-gray to silver-gray. Every shade of coat has a dark facial mask to emphasize the expression; color of the mask harmonizes with shade of body coat. Eyebrows, whiskers, cheeks, throat, chest, legs, and under tail are lighter in color but include "peppering." Markings are disqualifying faults.

Height: Height of withers of male is $25^1/_2$ to $27^1/_2$ inches (64.0–70.0 cm), and of female, $23^1/_2$ to $25^1/_2$ inches (60.0–65.0 cm), with the mediums being desired. Size alone should never take precedence over type, balance, soundness, and temperament. It should be noted that too small dogs generally lack the power and too large dogs, the agility and maneuverability desired in a working dog.

Scottish Terrier

The Scottish terrier, commonly known as the "Scottie," typifies the "Scottish-type": a long-bodied, low-slung, prick-eared terrier with a rough coat and fearless disposition. The breed has long inhabited Scotland's craggy mainland and is thought to have descended from the various working terrier strains that were common in the Highlands and also figured in the formation of the West Highland white, Dandie Dinmont, cairn, and Skye terriers.

From earliest times, the Scottish terrier was never limited to the traditional ratting function associated with most terriers, but also served as a hunting companion. Despite its smallness, the Scottie proved to be adept at retrieving from land and water and was used in various gundog capacities.

The breed is extremely well fixed in type and temperament. The Scottie stands 10 to 11 inches (25.4–28.0 cm) in height and weighs from 18 to 21

Scottish terriers, puppy and adult.

pounds (8.2–9.5 kg). The outer coat is very harsh and wiry, and the undercoat is quite dense. The tail is not docked and is carried upright. The overall impression is of a compact, well-muscled dog that packs a lot of strength into a small frame.

The Scottie is affectionate and playful toward its master, but it is every bit the game terrier when strangers or other dogs are involved. It will take on any dog, regardless of size, that invades its territory. While it can be good-natured and extremely tolerant of the antics of the children that share its household, it can be cold or even belligerent with anyone unfamiliar. It prefers to be a one-master dog. These qualities make Scotties able watchdogs, but the breed is not for everyone. A suitable owner must be willing to match wits with the stubbornness of this intelligent, self-confident dog and enforce some disciplinary guidelines. Obedience training and adequate vigorous exercise are highly recommended.

The Scottie's characteristic trim requires several trips to the grooming parlor each year, although interested fanciers can master the trimming techniques for a pet if guided by an experienced hand. Grooming for show involves plucking and limited trimming to retain the required harshness and flow of the coat. The coat should be brushed thoroughly every second day to prevent matting.

The breed is generally quite hardy and often lives to 14 or 15 years of age. Kidney stones can be a problem. Litters generally contain three to five puppies who quickly show great bone and a dense coat. Puppy socialization is especially important with the Scottie, as it can develop a sharp disposition if not shown a lot of affection while young.

Official Standard for the Scottish Terrier

Skull: Long, of medium width, slightly domed and covered with short, hard hair. Should not be quite flat; should be a slight stop or drop between eyes.

Muzzle: In proportion to length of skull, with not too much taper toward nose. Nose should be black and of good size. Jaws should be level and square. Nose projects somewhat over mouth, giving impression that upper jaw is longer than lower. Teeth should be evenly placed, having a scissors or level bite; the former preferable.

Eyes: Set wide apart, small and of almond shape, not round. Color dark brown or nearly black. Bright, piercing, and set well under brow.

Ears: Small, prick, set well up on skull, rather pointed but not cut. Hair on them should be short and velvety.

Neck: Moderately short, thick and muscular, strongly set on sloping shoulders, but not so short as to appear clumsy.

Chest: Broad and very deep, well let down between forelegs.

Body: Moderately short and well ribbed up with strong loin, deep flanks, and very muscular hindquarters.

Legs and Feet: Both forelegs and hind legs should be short and very heavy in bone in proportion to size of dog. Forelegs straight or slightly bent with elbows close to body. Scottish terriers should not be out at elbows. Stifles should be well bent and legs straight from hock to heel. Thighs very muscular. Feet round and thick with strong nails, forefeet larger than hind feet. *Note:* Gait of the Scottish terrier is peculiarly its own and very characteristic of the breed. It is not the square trot or walk that is desirable in the long-legged breeds. Forelegs do not move in exact parallel planes—rather in reaching out incline slightly inward. This is due to shortness of leg and width of chest. Action of rear legs should be square and true, and at the trot both hocks and stifles should be flexed with a vigorous motion.

Tail: Never cut and about 7 inches (18 cm) long, carried with a slight curve but not over the back.

Coat: Rather short, about 2 inches (5.1 cm), dense undercoat with outer coat intensely hard and wiry.

Size and Weight: Equal consideration must be given to height, length of back, and weight. Height at shoulder for either sex should be about 10 inches (25.4 cm). Generally, a well-balanced Scottish terrier dog of correct size should weigh from 19 to 22 pounds (8.6–10.0 kg) and a bitch, from 18 to 21 pounds (8.2–9.5 kg). The principal objective must be symmetry and balance.

Color: Steel or iron-gray, brindled or grizzled, black, sandy, or wheaten. White markings objectionable and can be allowed only on chest, and that to a slight extent only.

General Appearance: Face should wear a keen, sharp, and active expression. Both head and tail should be carried well up. Dog should look very compact, well muscled and powerful, giving the impression of immense power in a small size.

Description of Terrier Breeds

Sealyham Terrier

The Sealyham terrier originates from Wales in the 19th century, where it was utilized as a hunter of such cunning animals as foxes, weasels, and ferrets. This gives an indication of the courage of the breed, as it would fearlessly pursue and attack any predator. The Sealyham boasts a determination and eagerness for the hunt that is unsurpassed.

A variety of breeds is thought to figure in the Sealyham's background, including the white English terrier, the fox terrier, the Dandie Dinmont, and the bull terrier. The breed has endured through the years as a result of the efforts of sportsmen; it did not gain much attention as a show dog until the early part of the 1920s.

The characteristics of the breed include its white, wiry double coat, button ears, heavy eyebrows and whiskers, and short-coupled body. It stands approximately 10½ inches (27 cm) in height and weighs 22 to 24 pounds (10.0–10.9 kg). The tail is docked and carried upright.

Sealyham terriers, puppy and adult.

The Sealyham coat requires frequent trips to the groomer and considerable routine care to keep it looking tidy. Proper technique requires unruly hairs to be plucked; this requires a skilled hand. To prevent the coat from matting, it must be thoroughly combed through several times a week. The Sealyham also requires more bathing than is typical of other terriers, as its white coat comes in frequent contact with the ground and easily picks up and shows dirt.

The Sealyham terrier is generally well behaved in the home, and shows a distinctive sense of humor in its play. It retains a very youthful nature no matter what age it may be. It is most suited to a home with adults that can pay it a good deal of attention and allow it some vigorous exercise. A Sealyham is wary and suspicious of strangers, but not prone to aggressive outbursts. These characteristics make it a natural watchdog—alert enough to recognize danger yet not bothersome with noisy outbursts at every unusual sound. It is, however, the embodiment of spunk, so a good dose of discipline is required to counterbalance this dominant personality. Some Sealyhams can be antagonistic toward other dogs, especially males.

Like many of the all-white breeds, the Sealyham is sometimes prone to deafness and eye problems. Otherwise, it is quite long-lived. Litters generally contain from three to six puppies, which become very animated at a young age. Obedience training from early on is suggested.

Official Standard for the Sealyham Terrier

The Sealyham should be the embodiment of power and determination, ever keen and alert, of extraordinary substance, yet free from clumsiness.
Height: At withers about 10½ inches (26.9 cm).
Weight: 23 to 24 pounds (50.6–52.8 kg) for dogs; bitches slightly less. It should be borne in mind that size is more important than weight.

Description of Terrier Breeds

Head: Long, broad, and powerful, without coarseness; should, however, be in perfect balance with body, joining neck smoothly. Length of head roughly three-quarters height at withers, or about an inch (2.5 cm) longer than neck. Breadth between ears a little less than one-half length of head. *Skull:* Very slightly domed, with shallow indentation running down between brows, and joining muzzle with a moderate stop. *Cheeks:* Smoothly formed and flat, without heavy jowls. *Jaws:* Powerful and square. Bite level or scissors. *Teeth:* Sound, strong, and white, with canines fitting closely together. *Nose:* Black, with large nostrils. *Eyes:* Very dark, deeply set, and fairly wide apart, of medium size, oval in shape, with keen terrier expression. Lack of eye rim pigmentation not a fault. *Ears:* Folded level with top of head, with forward edge close to cheek. Well rounded at tip, and of length to reach outer corner of eye. Thin, not leathery, and of sufficient thickness to avoid creases.

Neck: Length slightly less than two-thirds of height of dog at withers. Muscular without coarseness, with good reach, refinement at throat, and set firmly on shoulders.

Shoulders: Well laid back and powerful, but not over-muscled. Sufficiently wide to permit freedom of action.

Legs: Forelegs strong, with good bone; and as straight as is consistent with chest being well let down between them. Hind legs longer than forelegs and not so heavily boned. *Feet:* Large but compact, round with thick pads, strong nails. Toes well arched and pointing straight ahead. Forefeet larger, though not quite so long as hind feet.

Body: Strong, short-coupled, and substantial, so as to permit great flexibility. Brisket deep and well let down between forelegs. Ribs well sprung.

Back: Length from withers to set-on of tail should approximate height at withers, or 10½ inches (27 cm). Topline level, neither roached nor swayed. *Hindquarters:* Very powerful, and protruding well behind the set-on of tail. Strong second thighs, stifles well bent, and hocks well let down.

Tail: Docked and carried upright. Set on far enough forward so that spine does not slope down to it.

Coat: Weather-resisting, comprised of soft, dense undercoat and hard, wiry top coat.

Color: All white, or with lemon, tan, or badger markings on head and ears.

Action: Sound, strong, quick, free, true, and level.

Silky Terrier

The silky terrier is another toy breed with a terrier heritage. It hails from Sydney, Australia, where it was derived from matings of Yorkshire terriers and Australian terriers. The breed was originally known as the Sydney silky and was often used to clear mice and rats from farmers' fields. The silky quicky gained popularity, as it sported the soft, lustrous coat of the Yorkie (but with little of the grooming requirements) yet maintained the true terrier spirit in a compact body.

Silky terriers, puppy and adult.

Description of Terrier Breeds

Today the silky terrier is assigned to the Toy Group, but don't let such a designation fool you. It is based primarily on size, not on temperament, for the silky could easily be placed in the Terrier Group for all its spunk, energy, and overall gameness. This toy breed does not take naturally to the life of a pampered lapdog, although it certainly loves affection and attention. The silky has a dominant personality and will try to take control of its environment if the owner is not wise to this tendency. Obedience training from an early age is suggested.

The silky is extremely protective of its home and master, perhaps taking this tendency a bit too far at times. While it makes a wonderful watchdog, the silky terrier tends to be a noisy, sometimes argumentative breed that does not care to share its home with other pets unless they are introduced early in life. The silky can get along amicably with children, if they are taught not to play roughly. This dog also has a natural desire to dart after any small animal it may spy, so it is advisable always to use a leash outdoors when the dog is not in a fenced area.

The silky terrier is normally a healthy, rather long-lived dog. It is not prone to many of the health or whelping problems of other toy breeds. It often lives 12 or more years and produces litters that normally average three to five puppies. The puppies should be monitored for possible tooth problems while growing. The silkies usually mature at around 18 to 24 months of age.

While not nearly as troublesome as the Yorkie's, the coat of the silky terrier will still need some grooming to keep it in good condition. To avoid matting, a daily brushing is strongly suggested. This moderate amount of work will help to foster the glossy coat that gives the breed its name and distinctive appearance.

Official Standard for the Silky Terrier

The silky terrier is a lightly built, moderately low-set toy dog of pronounced terrier character and spirited action.

Head: Strong, wedge-shaped, and moderately long. Skull a trifle longer than muzzle, in proportion about three-fifths for skull, two-fifths for muzzle. *Skull:* Flat, not too wide between ears. *Stop:* Shallow. *Ears:* Small, V-shaped and pricked. Set high and carried erect without any tendency to flare obliquely off skull. *Eyes:* Small, dark, and piercingly keen in expression. Light eyes are a fault. *Teeth:* Strong and well aligned, scissors bit. Bite markedly undershot or overshot is a serious fault. *Nose:* Black.

Neck and Shoulders: Fits gracefully into sloping shoulders. Medium long, fine, and to some degree crested along its topline.

Body: Low-set, about one fifth longer than dog's height at withers. A too short body is a fault. Back line is straight, with just perceptible rounding over loins. Brisket medium wide, and deep enough to extend down to elbows.

Tail: Set high and carried erect or semi-erect but not over-gay. Docked and well coated but devoid of plume.

Forequarters: Well laid back shoulders, together with good angulation at upper arm, set forelegs nicely under the body. Forelegs strong, straight, and rather fine-boned.

Hindquarters: Thighs well muscled and strong, but not so developed as to appear heavy. Legs moderately angulated at stifles and hocks, with hocks low and equidistant from hock joints to ground.

Feet: Small, catlike, round, compact. Pads are thick and springy while nails are strong and dark-colored. White or flesh-colored nails are a fault. Feet point straight ahead, with no turning in or out. Dewclaws, if any, are removed.

Coat: Flat, in texture fine, glossy, silky; on matured specimens desired length of coat from behind ears to set-on of tail is from 5 to 6 inches (12.7–15.3 cm). On top of head hair is so profuse as to form a topknot, but long hair on face and ears is objectionable. Legs from knee and hock joints to feet should be free from long hair. Hair is parted on head and down over back to root of tail.

Color: Blue and tan. The blue may be silver-blue, pigeon-blue or slate-blue, the tan deep and rich. The blue extends from base of skull to tip of tail, down forelegs to pasterns, and down thighs to hocks. On tail the blue should be very dark. Tan appears on muzzle and cheeks, around base of ears, below pasterns and hocks, and around vent. There is a tan spot over each eye. Topknot should be silver or fawn.

Temperament: The keenly alert air of the terrier is characteristic, with shyness or excessive nervousness to be faulted. Manner is quick, friendly, responsive.

Movement: Should be free, light-footed, lively, and straightforward. Hindquarters should have strong propelling power. Toeing in or out is to be faulted.

Size: Weight ranges from 8 to 10 pounds (3.6–4.5 kg). Shoulder height from 9 to 10 inches (23.0–25.4 cm). Pronounced diminutiveness, such as height of less than 8 inches (20.3 cm), is not desired; it accentuates the quality of toyishness as opposed to the breed's definite terrier character.

Skye Terrier

The Skye terrier is one of the oldest "Scottish-type" terriers; the breed is thought to date back to the 16th century, if not earlier. It is very long in body, while standing only 10 inches (25.4 cm) at the shoulder. The Skye terrier is, in fact, twice as long as it is high. It is covered with a profuse coat parted to fall straight down on either side of the body, while covering much of the face.

Skye terrier.

The coat is one of the most notable breed characteristics. It is double, with a soft, wooly undercoat and a hard, flat outer coat that reaches at least 5½ inches (14.0 cm) in length. It must be one color overall, but may have varying shades of the same color throughout the coat. Permissible colors are black, gray, blue, silver, cream, or fawn, and the ears are invariably black. Its legs are quite short and muscular, and it sports a long, well-feathered tail. Its ears can be either pricked or dropped.

The coat requires daily care if it is to reach its full potential. While it requires little or no trimming, it must be brushed and combed each day to prevent snarls, and requires frequent touch-up baths, since it picks up dirt as it brushes against the ground during movement. Most of the dirt is easily shed, however. A metal comb and a pin brush are most suited to the task. The hair around the mouth and rectum also needs frequent attention to remove all debris that can cling to the area.

In temperament, the Skye terrier is quite feisty and stubborn. While it can be extremely devoted to its master and even tolerant of children if raised with them, it can also be quite aggressive with outsiders. It is an avid watchdog and tends to be a bit noisy. The Skye terrier can be snappy when meeting other dogs and requires a good amount of obedience instruction. It is best suited for adults in one-dog households who have the interest and patience to give the coat the extensive attention it requires. Its exercise requirements are not substantial. Because of its long body length it does not do well in cramped quarters or in homes that require the dog to climb a lot of stairs.

The Skye terrier is a sturdy dog with good stamina. Litters have a wide range, and have been known to contain up to ten puppies. Puppies are born with a coat that is lighter than the adult coloring. It will normally clear to proper shadings by 18 months of age.

Official Standard for the Skye Terrier

General Appearance: The Skye terrier is a dog of style, elegance, and dignity; agile and strong with sturdy bone and hard muscle. Long, low, and lank—twice as long as high—covered with profuse coat that falls straight down either side of body over oval-shaped ribs. Hair well feathered on head veils forehead and eyes to serve as protection from brush and briar as well as amid serious encounters with other animals. Stands with head high and long tail hanging, and moves with a seemingly effortless gait. Of suitable size for hunting work, strong in body, quarters and jaw.

Temperament: That of typical working terrier capable of overtaking game and going to ground, displaying stamina, courage, strength, and agility. Fearless, good-tempered, loyal, and canny, friendly and gay with those it knows and reserved and cautious with strangers.

Head: Long and powerful, strength being deemed more important than extreme length. Moderate width at back of skull tapers gradually to strong muzzle. Stop is slight. Dark muzzle just moderately full as opposed to snipy; nose is always black. Powerful and absolutely true jaws and mouth with incisor teeth closing level, or with upper teeth slightly overlapping lower. *Eyes:* Brown, preferably dark brown, medium in size, close-set, and alight with life and intelligence. *Ears:* Symmetrical and gracefully feathered. May be carried prick or drop. When prick, medium in size, placed high on skull, erect at outer edges, and slightly wider apart at peak than at skull. Drop ears, somewhat larger in size and set lower, hang flat against skull.

Neck: Long and gracefully arched, carried high and proudly.

Body: Preeminently long and low. Backline is level, chest deep, with oval-shaped ribs. Sides appear flattish due to straight-falling and profuse coat.

Legs and Feet: *Forequarters:* Legs short, muscular, and straight as possible. "Straight as possible" means straight as soundness and chest will permit; it does not mean "terrier straight." Shoulders well laid back, with tight placement of shoulder blades at withers; elbows should fit closely to sides and be neither loose nor tied. Forearm should curve slightly around chest. *Hindquarters:* Strong, full, well developed, and well angulated. Legs short, muscular, and straight when viewed from behind. *Feet:* Large harefeet preferably pointing forward, pads thick and nails strong and preferably black.

Description of Terrier Breeds

Movement: Legs proceed straight forward when traveling. When approaching, forelegs form a continuation of the straight line of front, feet being same distance apart as elbows. Principal propelling power is furnished by hind legs, which travel straight forward. Forelegs should move well forward without too much lift. Whole movement may be termed free, active, and effortless, and give a more or less fluid picture.

Tail: Long and well feathered. When hanging, upper section is pendulous, following line of rump, its lower section thrown back in a moderate arc without twist or curl. When raised, its height makes it appear a prolongation of backline. Though not to be preferred, tail is sometimes carried high when dog is excited or angry. When such carriage arises from emotion only, it is permissible. But tail should not be constantly carried above level of back nor hang limp.

Coat: Double. Undercoat short, close, soft, and woolly. Outer coat hard, straight, and flat, 5½ inches (14.0 cm) long, without extra credit granted for greater length. Body coat hangs straight down each side, parting from head to tail. Head hair, which may be shorter and softer, veils forehead and eyes and forms a moderate beard and apron. Long feathering on ears falls straight down from tips and outer edges, surrounding ears like a fringe and outlining their shape. Ends of hair should mingle with coat at sides of neck.

Color: Coat must be one overall color at the skin but may be of varying shades of same color in full coat, which may be black, blue, dark or light gray, silver-platinum, fawn, or cream. Dog must have no distinctive markings except for the desirable black points of ears, muzzle, and tip of tail, all of which points are preferably dark even to black. Shade of head and legs should approximate that of body. There must be no trace of pattern, design, or clear-cut color variations, with the exception of the breed's only permissible white which occasionally exists on chest not exceeding 2 inches (5.1 cm) in diameter.

The puppy coat may be very different in color from the adult coat. As it is growing and clearing, wide variations of color may occur; consequently this is permissible in dogs under 18 months of age. However, even in puppies there must be no trace of pattern, design, or clear-cut variations with the exception of black band of varying width frequently seen encircling body coat of cream-colored dog, and the only permissible white which, as in adult dog, occasionally exists on chest, not exceeding 2 inches (5.1 cm) in diameter.

Size: Dogs: Shoulder height, 10 inches (25.4 cm). Length, chest bone over tail at rump, 20 inches (51.0 cm). Head, 8½ inches (22.0 cm). Tail 9 inches (23 cm). Bitches: Shoulder height, 9½ inches (24.1 cm). Length, chest bone over tail at rump, 19 inches (48.3 cm). Head, 8 inches (20.3 cm). Tail 8½ inches (22.0 cm). A slightly higher or lower dog of either sex is acceptable, providing body, head, and tail dimensions are proportionately longer or shorter. Ideal ratio of body length to shoulder height is 2 to 1, which is considered the correct proportion.

Measurements are taken with the Skye standing in natural position with feet well under. A box caliper is used vertically and horizontally. For height, top bar should rest on withers. Head is measured from tip of nose to back of occipital bone, and tail from root to tip. Dogs 8 inches (20.3 cm) or less at withers and bitches 7½ inches (19.1 cm) or less at withers are to be penalized.

Soft-Coated Wheaten Terrier

Southern Ireland is the homeland of the soft-coated wheaten. It is believed to be the oldest of the Irish terriers, dating back more than 200 years and a likely ancestor of the Kerry blue terrier. The breed owes its name to the ripe-wheat color of its coat. While this breed originally functioned as most other terriers in ridding the fields of small vermin, it also showed great ability as a sporting dog in the hunt and as a herder of cattle.

Soft-coated wheaten terrier.

The soft-coated wheaten is a medium-sized dog, standing to 19 inches (48.3 cm) at the withers and weighing between 35–45 pounds (15.9–20.4 kg). It has button ears, dark eyes, and a docked tail. The abundant, naturally wavy coat is the highlight of the breed. It is a clear wheaten color, soft in texture, and sheds little.

Unlike many of its terrier cousins, the soft-coated wheaten does not exhibit many aggressive tendencies, even toward other household pets. It gets along peacefully and cheerfully with everyone, and can be trusted to play alone with children.

It is a quick and avid learner that rarely fails to cooperate with its owner's wishes. The breed thrives when allowed vigorous exercise, but can still be raised within the confines of a city or apartment. It is a people-oriented breed that does not do well when confined alone for long stretches of time. Several walks a day will suffice to keep the dog in good trim. It is a natural watchdog, but not prone to continuous barking.

The wheaten's coat requires a great deal of attention but it should not be extensively trimmed. For show purposes, it can be tidied with thinning shears, but clipping, plucking, and styling are not allowed. To avoid snarls, the coat should be combed through at least every other day with a wide-toothed metal comb and a slicker brush that will not rip out the hairs.

The profuse coat of the wheaten may sometimes mask skin allergies, but otherwise it is a healthy breed. There are few whelping problems, and litters generally contain five or more puppies. The newborns will be born with coats that are darker than the adult shade, but this will usually be resolved by 18 to 24 months of age.

Official Standard for the Soft-Coated Wheaten Terrier

General Appearance: The soft-coated wheaten terrier is a medium-sized hardy, well-balanced sporting terrier, square in outline. Distinguished by soft, silky, gently waving coat of warm wheaten color and particularly steady disposition. Breed requires moderation both in structure and in presentation; any exaggerations are to be shunned. Should present overall appearance of an alert and happy animal, graceful, strong, and well-coordinated.

Head: Well balanced and in proportion to body. Rectangular in appearance; moderately long. Powerful with no suggestion of coarseness.
Skull: Flat and clean between ears. Cheekbones not prominent. Defined stop. Skull and foreface

of equal length. *Muzzle:* Powerful and strong, well filled below the eyes. No suggestion of snipiness. Lips tight and black. *Nose:* Black and large for size of dog. *Eyes:* Dark reddish brown or brown, medium in size, slightly almond shaped, and set fairly wide apart. Eye rims black. *Ears:* Small to medium in size, breaking level with skull and dropping slightly forward, inside edge of ear lying next to cheek and pointing to ground rather than to eye. *Teeth:* Large, clean, and white; scissors or level bite.

Neck: Medium in length, clean and strong, not throaty. Carried proudly, it gradually widens, blending smoothly into the body.

Shoulders: Well laid back, clean and smooth; well knit.

Body: Compact; back strong and level; relatively short coupled. Ribs well sprung but without roundness; chest deep. Tail docked and well set on, carried gaily but never over back.

Legs and Feet: Forelegs straight and well boned. Hind legs well developed with well-bent stifles turned neither in nor out; hocks well let down and parallel to each other. *Feet:* round and compact with good depth of pad. Nails dark; pads black. All *dewclaws* should be removed.

Coat: A distinguishing characteristic of the breed which sets the dog apart from all other terriers. An abundant single coat covering entire body, legs and head; coat on the head falls forward to shade the eyes. Texture soft and silky with a gentle wave. *Color:* Any shade of wheaten. Upon close examination, occasional red, white, or black guard hairs may be found. However, overall coloring must be clearly wheaten with no evidence of any other color except on ears and muzzle, where blue-gray shading is sometimes present. *Puppies and Adolescents:* Puppies under a year may carry deeper coloring and occasional black tipping. The adolescent, under two years, often quite light in color, but must never be white or carry gray other than on ears and muzzle. However, by two years of age,

the *proper* wheaten color should be obvious. In both puppies and adolescents, mature wavy coat is generally not yet evident.

Size: A dog shall be 18 to 19 inches (46.0–48.3 cm) at withers, ideal being 18½ inches (47.0 cm). A bitch shall be 17 to 18 inches (43.2–46.0 cm) at withers, ideal being 17½ inches (44.5 cm). Dogs should weigh 35 to 40 pounds (15.9–18.1 kg); bitches 30 to 35 pounds (13.6–15.9 kg).

Movement: Gait is free, graceful, and lively, with good reach in front and strong drive behind. Front and rear feet turn neither in nor out.

Temperament: The wheaten is a happy, steady dog and shows himself gaily with an air of self-confidence. Alert, exhibits interest in surroundings; exhibits less aggressiveness than is sometimes encouraged in other terriers. Dogs who fail to keep their tails erect when moving should be severely penalized.

Presentation: For show purposes, the wheaten is presented to show a terrier outline, but coat must be of sufficient length to flow when dog is in motion. Coat must never be clipped or plucked. Sharp contrasts or stylizations must be avoided. Headcoat should be blended to present a rectangular outline. Eyes should be indicated but never fully exposed. Ears should be relieved of fringe, but not taken down to leather. Sufficient coat must be left on skull, cheeks, neck, and tail to balance proper length of body coat.

A miniature schnauzer that has been trained to "sit" and "come" on command.

Staffordshire Bull Terrier

The Staffordshire bull terrier, along with its larger cousin, the American Staffordshire terrier, finds itself in the unenviable position of having to defend itself against a public image of a crazed "pit bull terrier." This image does not do justice to a breed that is, in fact, very affectionate and intelligent. Well-bred, well-trained Staffordshire bull terriers are not synonymous with the vicious creatures commonly termed "pit bulls." Such unfortunate animals are almost always the products of improper mixed breedings (using the most vicious parents possible) and improper training (being deprived of honest affection and discipline). Many are *taught* to be mean.

Staffordshire bull terriers, puppy and adult.

The largest of the terriers: The Airedale (top) and the giant schnauzer (bottom).

The Staffordshire bull terrier hails from northern England, where, in ages long since past, large, muscular dogs of more than 100 pounds were regularly used in the "sport" of dogfighting. Over time, these early relatives of today's mastiff and bulldog were gradually down-sized through selective breeding. Dogfighting reached a peak in the mid-19th century when crosses with working terrier strains were introduced to give the resulting dogs greater speed and agility. The result was a Staffordshire bull terrier—35 pounds (15.9 kg) of sheer courage, tenacity, and an extremely punishing bite.

This "sport" was eventually outlawed and breeders discovered that by raising this dog with discipline and affection rather than instruction in viciousness, it became a very personable canine associate. Over the years the Stafforshire bull terrier has proven itself to be an extremely loyal, affectionate breed that is quite popular as a companion in the home. A Staffordshire terrier that has been raised with an ample amount of obedience training and affection will be very devoted and gentle toward its master. Its effectiveness as a watchdog is superb.

Today's Staffordshire bull terrier is an extremely muscular breed that imparts an immediate impression of strength and power. It has a long, undocked tail and a smooth coat, which can be found in a variety of colors. It stands approximately 16 inches (41 cm) at the shoulder and weighs 24 to 34 pounds (10.9–15.4 kg).

This breed is generally hardy and healthy, although cases of tumors and a tendency toward hip dysplasia have been reported. Litters generally contain five or more puppies.

People considering owning this breed have a responsibility to give it ample exercise and obedience training. It should not be allowed to roam free. This breed does not get along well with other pets in the household.

Description of Terrier Breeds

Official Standard for the Staffordshire Bull Terrier

Characteristics: From the past history of the Staffordshire bull terrier, the modern dog draws its character of indomitable courage, high intelligence, and tenacity. This, coupled with its affection for its friends, and children in particular, its off-duty quietness and trustworthy stability, makes it a foremost all-purpose dog.

General Appearance: The Staffordshire bull terrier is smooth-coated. Should be of great strength for its size and, although muscular, should be active and agile.

Head and Skull: Short, deep through, broad skull, very pronounced cheek muscles, distinct stop, short foreface, black nose. *Eyes:* Dark preferable, but may bear some relation to coat color. Round, of medium size, and set to look straight ahead. Light eyes or pink eye rims to be considered a fault, except that where coat surrounding eye is white the eye rim may be pink. *Ears:* Rose or half-pricked and not large. *Mouth:* A bite in which outer side of lower incisors touches inner side of upper incisors. Lips should be tight and clean.

Neck: Muscular, rather short, clean in outline, and gradually widening toward shoulders.

Forequarters: Legs straight and well boned, set rather far apart, without looseness at shoulders and showing no weakness at pasterns, from which point feet turn out a little.

Body: Close coupled, with level topline, wide front, deep brisket, and well-sprung ribs rather light in loins.

Hindquarters: Should be well muscled, hocks let down with stifles well bent. Legs should be parallel when viewed from behind.

Feet: Should be well padded, strong, and of medium size. Dewclaws, if any, on hind legs generally removed. Dewclaws on forelegs may be removed.

Tail: Undocked, of medium length, low set, tapering to a point, and carried rather low. Should not curl much and may be likened to an old-fashioned pump handle.

Coat: Smooth, short, and close to the skin, not to be trimmed or dewhiskered. *Color:* Red, fawn, white, black or blue, or any of these colors with white. Any shade of brindle or any shade of brindle with white.

Size: Weight: Dogs, 28 to 38 pounds (12.7–17.2 kg); bitches, 24 to 34 pounds (10.9–15.4 kg). Height at shoulder: 14 to 16 inches (36.0–41.0 cm), these heights being related to weights.

Welsh Terrier

As the name implies, the homeland of the Welsh terrier is Wales. This very old breed has been kept true to type for at least 100 years. The effect of earlier crosses of the Old English terrier, as it was originally known, with the wire fox terrier produced a compact, medium-sized dog of great stamina and intelligence, capable of hunting the fox, otter, or badger.

Welsh terrier.

Description of Terrier Breeds

The Welsh terrier stands about 15 inches (38.4 cm) at the withers and weighs approximately 20 pounds (44 kg). Its coat is hard, wiry, and very abundant. The color is a rich black and tan. Its tail is docked to a medium length and is carried upright. The ears are folded just above the top of the skull.

The personality of the Welsh terrier is very well rounded, having the inborn spunk and tenacity of the typical terrier but lacking much of the aggressiveness. It gets along agreeably with everyone— including other dogs—and has a natural desire to please. It will never shy away from a challenge, however, as it is extremely courageous.

The Welsh takes obedience instruction with a more positive attitude than many of the more stubborn terriers. The breed's intelligence is apparent in any task it undertakes, and it has had considerable success in obedience competition.

In the home, the Welsh terrier is a fine, loyal companion that is trustworthy around children. While not overly vocal, it is instinctively attentive to all that goes on around it and is a natural watchdog. It is clean and does not need much grooming. Regular brushing and the plucking of stray hairs will generally keep the coat neat, while the typical facial expression is achieved through some careful trimming. An experienced breeder or groomer can teach the interested fancier how to achieve the desired look at home.

Welsh terriers are quite hardy, but may occasionally develop skin irritations, especially if external parasites are allowed to penetrate the dense coat. The normal litter size is from three to six puppies.

Official Standard for the Welsh Terrier

General Appearance: The Welsh terrier is a sturdy, compact rugged dog of medium size with a coarse wire-textured coat. Legs, underbody, and head are tan; jacket black (or occasionally grizzle). Tail is docked to length meant to complete the image of a "square dog" approximately as high as long. Movement is a terrier trot typical of long-legged terrier; effortless, with good reach and drive. The Welsh terrier is friendly, outgoing to people and other dogs, showing spirit and courage. Intelligence and desire to please are evident in attitude. The "Welsh terrier expression" comes from the set, color, and position of the eyes combined with use of ears.

Head: Entire head is rectangular. Foreface is strong with powerful, punishing jaws. Only slightly narrower than backskull. There is a slight stop. Backskull is of equal length to foreface. They are on parallel planes in profile. Backskull is smooth and flat (not domed) between ears. No wrinkles between ears. Cheeks flat and clean (not bulging). *Muzzle:* One-half the length of entire head from tip of nose to occiput. Foreface in front of eyes well made up. Furnishings on foreface trimmed to complete— without exaggeration—the total rectangular outline. Muzzle is strong and squared off, never snipy. Lips are black and tight. *Nose:* Black and squared off. *Teeth:* Scissors bite preferred, but level bite acceptable. Either one has complete dentition. Teeth large and strong, set in powerful, vicelike jaws. *Eyes:* Small, dark brown, and almond-shaped, well set in skull. Placed fairly far apart. Size, shape, color and position of eyes give the steady, confident, but alert expression typical of the Welsh terrier. *Ears:* V-shaped, small, but not too thin. Fold is just above topline of skull. Ears are carried forward close to cheek with tips falling to, or toward, outside corners of eyes when dog is at rest. Ears move slightly up and forward when at attention.

Description of Terrier Breeds

Neck: Of moderate length and thickness, slightly arched and sloping gracefully into shoulders. Throat clean with no excess of skin.

Body: Shows good substance, is well ribbed up with level topline. Loin is strong and moderately short. Good depth of brisket and moderate width of chest. Front is straight. Shoulders are long, sloping, and well laid back.

Forelegs and Feet: Legs are straight and muscular with upright and powerful pasterns. Feet are small, round, catlike. Pads are thick and black. Nails are strong and black. Dewclaws (front and back) are removed.

Hindquarters: Strong and muscular with well-developed second thighs and stifles well bent. Hocks are moderately straight, parallel, and short from joint to ground.

Tail: Docked to a length approximately level (on an imaginary line) with occiput, to complete square image of the whole dog. Root of tail set well up on back; carried upright.

Movement: Straight, free, and effortless, with good reach in front, strong drive behind, with feet naturally tending to converge toward a median line of travel as speed increases.

Coat: Hard, wiry, and dense, with a close-fitting, thick jacket. Short, soft undercoat. Furnishings on muzzle, legs, and quarters dense and wiry. *Color:* Jacket is black, spreading up onto neck, down onto tail, and into upper thighs. Legs, quarters, and head clear tan. Tan is deep reddish brown with slightly lighter shades acceptable. Grizzle jacket also acceptable.

Size: Males about 15 inches (38.1 cm) at withers, with acceptable range between 15 and 15¹/₂ inches (38.1–39.3 cm). Bitches may be proportionally smaller. Twenty pounds (9.1 kg) considered average weight, varying a few pounds depending on height of dog and density of bone. Both dog and bitch appear solid and of good substance.

Temperament: The Welsh terrier is a game dog—alert, aware, spirited—but at the same time, is friendly and shows self-control. A specimen exhibiting an overly aggressive attitude, or shyness, should be penalized.

West Highland White Terrier

The West Highland white terrier has been present throughout Scotland for hundreds of years. It traces back to the native terrier stock that also served as ancestor of the Scottish, Dandie Dinmont, cairn, and Skye terriers. The "Westie," as it is commonly known, had the perfect conformation for work among the hills and crevices of the Scottish Highlands. Its compact body allowed it to go to the earth after its prey, and it was nimble enough to navigate the rocks while trailing after a fox, badger, or otter. It demonstrated a natural cunning and intelligence unsurpassed by the other terrier breeds.

West Highland white terriers, puppy and adult.

Description of Terrier Breeds

The striking white coat of the Westie, as contrasted with its jet black nose, is the breed's most notable trait. The harsh double coat grows to about 2 inches (5.1 cm) in length. There is an abundance of hair on the face. Despite its color, the coat is not overly difficult to maintain, since a hard coat easily releases dirt. The coat should be thoroughly combed every other day and routinely trimmed around the edges to keep the ends tidy. The breed is to be shown "naturally," and the coat does not require extensive shaping. A show dog must have its coat plucked and stripped, but owners of pet Westies can attend to its needs by clipping or shaping with scissors. This will soften up the desired harsh outer coat texture, however, and make it more susceptible to retaining dirt.

The Westie packs a lot of terrier into a small frame, as it stands only 10 to 11 inches (25.4–28.0 cm) at the withers and weighs approximately 18 to 19 pounds (8.2–8.6 kg). Its legs are slightly longer than the other "Scottish-type" terriers. Its penetrating dark eyes and erect ears help give the breed an especially keen expression.

With an average life expectancy of 12 to 14 years, the Westie has proven itself to be a robust terrier. It is prone to some skin disorders, however. The average litter size is three to five puppies, which are born white but with pink markings on the nose and footpads. These points will blacken in several months.

Temperamentally, the Westie makes a fine companion for all ages. It is affectionate and playful; it will peacefully tolerate the presence of other animals in the house, but probably not be enthusiastic about this. It is a natural watchdog, and may carry this to an extreme by being *too* vocal. If confined for any length of time, it may also react with tireless barking. This can be controlled if corrected while young. The Westie is also an avid digger; this is a natural instinct that is hard to control. Its stamina enables it to keep pace with the most avid outdoorsman, and ample exercise is advisable. Be sure to have deep-set fencing in your Westie's outside area, as it is a renowned escape artist.

Official Standard for the West Highland White Terrier

General Appearance: The West Highland white terrier is a small, game, well-balanced, hardy-looking terrier, exhibiting good showmanship, possessed with no small amount of self-esteem, strongly built, deep in chest and back ribs; straight back and powerful hindquarters on muscular legs, and exhibiting in marked degree a great combination of strength and activity. Coat should be about 2 inches (5.1 cm) long, white, hard, with plenty of soft undercoat. The dog should be neatly presented. Considerable hair should be left around head to act as frame for face to yield a typical Westie expression.

Color and Pigmentation: Coat should be white, as defined by the breed's name. Nose should be black. Black pigmentation is most desirable on lips, eye rims, pads of feet, nails and skin.

Coat: Very important and seldom seen to perfection; must be double-coated. Outer coat consists of straight hard hair, about 2 inches long (5.1 cm), with shorter coat on neck and shoulders, properly blended.

Size: Dogs should measure about 11 inches (28.0 cm) at withers, bitches about 1 inch (2.5 cm) less.

Skull: Should be fairly broad, in proportion to powerful jaw, not too long, slightly domed, and gradually tapering to eyes. Should be a defined stop, eyebrows heavy.

Muzzle: Should be slightly shorter than skull, powerful, gradually tapering to nose, which should be large. Jaws should be level and powerful, teeth well set and large for size of dog. There should be six incisor teeth between canines of both lower and upper jaws. Tight scissors bite with upper incisors slighly overlapping lower incisors or level mouth are equally acceptable.

Ears: Small, carried tightly erect, set wide apart and terminating in a sharp point. Must never be cropped. Hair on ears should be short, smooth, and velvety, and trimmed free of fringe at tips.

Eyes: Widely set apart, medium in size, dark in color, slightly sunk in head, sharp and intelligent. Looking from under heavy eyebrows, they give a piercing look.

Neck: Muscular and nicely set on sloping shoulders.

Chest: Very deep and extending at least to elbows with breadth in proportion to size of dog.

Body: Compact and of good substance, level back, ribs deep and well arched in upper half of rib, presenting flattish side appearance, loins broad and strong, hindquarters strong, muscular, and wide across top.

Legs and Feet: Both forelegs and hind legs should be muscular and relatively short, but with sufficient length to set the dog up so as not to be too close to the ground. Shoulder blades should be well laid back and well knit at backbone. Chest should be relatively broad and front legs spaced apart accordingly. Front legs should be set in under shoulder blades with definite body overhang before them. Front legs should be reasonably straight and thickly covered with short hard hair. Hind legs should be short and sinewy; thighs very muscular and not set wide apart, with hocks well bent. Forefeet are larger than hind ones, are round, proportionate in size, strong, thickly padded, and covered with short hard hair; they may properly be turned out a slight amount. Hind feet are smaller and thickly padded.

Tail: Relatively short, when standing erect it should never extend above top of skull. Should be covered with hard hairs, no feather, as straight as possible, carried gaily but not curled over back. Tail should be set on high enough so that spine does not slope down to it. Tail must never be docked.

Movement: Should be free, straight, and easy all around. In front, leg should be freely extended forward by shoulder. Hind movement should be free, strong, and fairly close. Hocks should be freely flexed and drawn close under body; so that when moving off foot the body is thrown or pushed forward with some force.

Temperament: Must be alert, gay, courageous, and self-reliant, but friendly.

Yorkshire Terrier

This diminutive member of the Toy Group can trace its heritage to various terrier strains common to Scotland and England in the 19th century. Despite its small stature, the breed can be as persevering and feisty as any of its larger relations. The Yorkie was originally known as the Scottish terrier, a name which was shed once the breed became the favorite of the coal miners in the Yorkshire area. There these dogs, used to rid the mine shafts of mice and other small vermin, earned a reputation for being steadfast, dependable workers.

Yorkshire terriers, puppy and adult.

Description of Terrier Breeds

The Yorkshire terrier is one of the most popular toy breeds, owing largely to its lustrous, silky coat. When properly maintained, the coat can grow to beyond floor length. This regal appearance has made it a popular, fashionable pet. Fashion is not without a price, however. The Yorkie's coat requires vigilant, daily attention to reach its potential. Those Yorkshire terriers destined for the show ring will require constant monitoring for potential damage to the coat and will generally require that the coat be kept in wrappers.

The Yorkshire terrier enjoys the life of lapdog and can be extremely affectionate toward its master. It will get along well with other house pets, but flourishes best when allowed to "rule the roost." The typical Yorkie makes a fine watchdog, with a keen sense of hearing, a lively bark, and above average intelligence.

Most Yorkshire terriers weigh 2 to 7 pounds (0.9–3.2 kg). Such a tiny, compact body can entail some physical problems. Many Yorkie bitches are too small to whelp puppies naturally, making them likely candidates for cesarean sections and life-threatening births.

The average litter size is two to four, with all the puppies being born black with tan markings. As the puppy grows, the black hairs will be shed and replaced by the straight, silky, steel-blue or tan hairs that are the highlight of the breed. Eye and tooth problems are also common to the breed and the overall health of the dog must be routinely monitored from the time it is a puppy. The Yorkie is slow to mature and will take at least two years to attain its adult stature.

Although most Yorkies are not unusually frail, some owners feel it is best not to risk illness by exposing these dogs to the extremes of the various seasons—be it the heat of summer or the cold of winter—so they often keep their Yorkie paper-trained throughout its life. Since the breed is generally quite active around the house, little formal exercise is needed.

It should never be forgotten that a terrier heritage is basic to the Yorkshire terrier. It can be an extremely assertive breed, determined to have its own way. This strong will is often enhanced by owners who treat the Yorkie more like a pampered child than a dog—constantly carrying it, grooming it, and habitually doting on its care. If left unchecked, the dog's willfulness can result in destructive behavior when the Yorkie is left unattended. A moderate dose of obedience training will do much to temper the will of the Yorkshire terrier and mold it into a superior house pet.

Official Standard for the Yorkshire Terrier

General Appearance: That of a long-haired toy terrier whose blue and tan coat is parted on the face and from base of skull to end of tail and hangs evenly and quite straight down each side of body. Body is neat, compact, and well proportioned. Dog's high head carriage and confident manner should give the appearance of vigor and self-importance.

Head: Small and rather flat on top. *Skull* not too prominent or round. *Muzzle* not too long. *Bite* neither undershot nor overshot and teeth sound. Either scissors bite or level bite is acceptable. *Nose* is black. *Eyes* medium in size and not too prominent; dark in color and sparkling with a sharp, intelligent expression. Eye rims dark. *Ears* small, V-shaped, carried erect, and set not too far apart.

Body: Well proportioned and very compact. Back rather short, back line level, with height at shoulder same as at rump.

Legs and Feet: *Forelegs* should be straight, elbows neither in nor out. *Hind legs* straight when viewed from behind, but stifles moderately bent when viewed from sides. *Feet* round with black toenails. Dewclaws, if any, are generally removed from hind legs. Dewclaws on forelegs may be removed.

Tail: Docked to medium length and carried slightly higher than level of back.

Coat: Quality, texture, and quantity of coat of prime importance. Hair glossy, fine, and silky in texture. Coat on body moderately long and perfectly straight (not wavy). May be trimmed to floor length to give east of movement and a neater appearance, if desired. Fall on the head is long, tied with one bow in center of head or parted in middle and tied with two bows. Hair on muzzle very long. Hair should be trimmed short on tips of ears and may be trimmed on feet to give them a neat appearance.

Colors: Puppies are born black and tan and are normally darker in body color, showing an intermingling of black hair in the tan until they are matured. Color of hair on body and richness of tan on head and legs of prime importance in *adult dogs,* to which the following color requirements apply: *Blue:* Is a dark steel-blue, not a silver-blue and not mingled with fawn, bronzy, or black hairs. *Tan:* All tan hair is darker at roots than in middle, shading to still lighter tan at tips. There should be no sooty or black hair intermingled with any of the tan. *Color on Body:* The blue extends over body from back of neck to root of tail. Hair on tail is a darker blue, especially at end of tail. *Headfall.* A rich golden tan, deeper in color at sides of head, at ear roots and on the muzzle, with ears a deep rich tan. Tan color should not extend down on back of neck. *Chest and Legs:* A bright, rich tan, not extending above elbow on forelegs nor above stifle on hind legs.

Weight: Must not exceed 7 pounds (3.2 kg).

Index

Index

Index

Perfect for Pet Owners!

"Clear, concise...written in simple, nontechnical language."

—*Booklist*

AFRICAN GRAY PARROTS Wolter (3773-1)
AMAZON PARROTS Lantermann (4035-X)
BANTAMS Fritzsche (3687-5)
BEAGLES Vriends-Parent (9017-9)
BEEKEEPING Melzer (4089-9)
BOSTON TERRIERS Bulanda (1696-3)
BOXERS Kraupa-Tuskany (4036-8)
CANARIES Frisch (4611-0)
CATS Fritzsche (4442-8)
CHINCHILLAS Röder-Thiede (1471-5)
CHOW-CHOWS Atkinson (3952-1)
COCKATIELS Wolter (2889-9)
COCKATOOS Lantermann & Lantermann (4159-3)
COCKER SPANIELS Sucher (1478-2)
COLLIES Sundstrom & Sundstrom (1875-3)
CONURES Vriends (4880-6)
DACHSHUNDS Fiedelmeier (1843-5)
DALMATIANS Ditto (4605-6)
DISCUS FISH Giovanette (4669-2)
DOBERMAN PINSCHERS Gudas (9015-2)
DOGS Wegler (4822-9)
DOVES Vriends (1855-9)
DWARF RABBITS Wegler (1352-2)
ENGLISH SPRINGER SPANIELS Ditto (1778-1)
FEEDING AND SHELTERING BACKYARD BIRDS
   Vriends (4252-2)
FEEDING AND SHELTERING EUROPEAN BIRDS
   von Frisch (2858-9)
FERRETS Morton (9021-7)
GERBILS Gudas (9020-9)
GERMAN SHEPHERDS Antesberger (2982-8)
GOLDEN RETRIEVERS Sucher (9019-5)
GOLDFISH Ostrow (9016-0)
GREAT DANES Stahlkuppe (1418-9)
GUINEA PIGS Bielfeld (4612-9)
GUPPIES, MOLLIES, PLATYS
   Hieronimus (1497-9)
HAMSTERS Fritzsche (4439-8)
IRISH SETTERS Stahlkuppe (4663-3)
KEESHONDEN Stahlkuppe (1560-6)

LABRADOR RETRIEVERS Kern (9018-7)
LHASA APSOS Wehrman (3950-5)
LIZARDS IN THE TERRARIUM Jes (3925-4)
LONGHAIRED CATS Müller (2803-1)
LONG-TAILED PARAKEETS Wolter (1351-4)
LORIES AND LORIKEETS Vriends (1567-3)
LOVEBIRDS Vriends (9014-4)
MACAWS Sweeney (4768-0)
MICE Bielfeld (2921-6)
MINIATURE PIGS Storer (1356-5)
MUTTS Frye (4126-7)
MYNAHS von Frisch (3688-3)
NONVENOMOUS SNAKES Trutnau (5632-9)
PARAKEETS Wolter (4437-1)
PARROTS Wolter (4823-7)
PERSIAN CATS Müller (4405-3)
PIGEONS Vriends (4044-9)
POMERANIANS Stahlkuppe (4670-6)
PONIES Kraupa-Tuskany (2856-2)
POODLES Ullmann & Ullmann (2812-0)
PUGS Maggitti (1824-9)
RABBITS Fritzsche (4440-1)
RATS Himsel (4535-1)
SCHNAUZERS Frye (3949-1)
SCOTTISH FOLD CATS Maggitti (4999-3)
SHAR-PEI Ditto (4834-2)
SHEEP Müller (4091-0)
SHETLAND SHEEPDOGS Sucher (4264-6)
SIAMESE CATS Collier (4764-8)
SIBERIAN HUSKIES Kenn (4265-4)
SMALL DOGS Kriechbaumer (1951-2)
SNAKES Griehl (2813-9)
SPANIELS Ullmann & Ullmann (2424-9)
TROPICAL FISH Stadelmann (4700-1)
TURTLES Wilke (4702-8)
WEST HIGHLAND WHITE TERRIERS
   Bolle-Kleinbub (1950-4)
YORKSHIRE TERRIERS Kriechbaumer & Grünn
   (4406-1)
ZEBRA FINCHES Martin (3497-X)

Paperback, 6½ x 7⅞ with over 50 illustrations (20-plus color photos)

Barron's ISBN prefix: 0-8120

Barron's Educational Series, Inc. • 250 Wireless Blvd., Hauppauge, NY 11788
Call toll-free: 1-800-645-3476 • In Canada: Georgetown Book Warehouse
34 Armstrong Ave., Georgetown, Ont. L7G 4R9 • Call toll-free: 1-800-247-7160

Order these titles from your favorite book or pet store.

(#61) R7/95

BARRON'S PET REFERENCE BOOKS

Barron's Pet Reference Books are and have long been the choice of experts and discerning pet owners. Why? Here are just a few reasons. These indispensable volumes are packed with 35 to 200 stunning full-color photos. Each provides the very latest expert information and answers questions that pet owners often wonder about.

BARRON'S PET REFERENCE BOOKS ARE:

AQUARIUM FISH (1350-6)
AQUARIUM FISH BREEDING (4474-6)
THE AQUARIUM FISH SURVIVAL MANUAL (9391-7)
BEFORE YOU BUY THAT PUPPY (1750-1)
THE BEST PET NAME BOOK EVER (4258-1)
CARING FOR YOUR SICK CAT (1726-9)
THE COMPLETE BOOK OF BUDGERIGARS (6059-8)
THE CAT CARE MANUAL (1767-6)
CIVILIZING YOUR PUPPY (4953-5)
COMMUNICATING WITH YOUR DOG (4203-4)
THE COMPLETE BOOK OF CAT CARE (4613-7)
THE COMPLETE BOOK OF DOG CARE (4158-5)
THE DOG CARE MANUAL (9163-9)

GOLDFISH AND ORNAMENTAL CARP (9286-4)
GUIDE TO HOME PET GROOMING (4298-0)
HEALTHY CAT, HAPPY CAT (9136-1)
HEALTHY DOG, HAPPY DOG (1842-7)
HOP TO IT: A Guide to Training Your Pet Rabbit (4551-3)
THE HORSE CARE MANUAL (1133-3)
HOW TO TEACH YOUR OLD DOG NEW TRICKS (4544-0)
LABYRINTH FISH (5635-3)
THE COMPLETE BOOK OF MACAWS (9037-3)
NONVENOMOUS SNAKES (5632-9)
TROPICAL MARINE FISH SURVIVAL MANUAL (9372-0)
SECRET LIFE OF CATS, THE (6513-1)

Barron's Educational Series, Inc., 250 Wireless Boulevard, Hauppauge, New York 11788. For faster service call toll-free: 1-800-645-3476.

In Canada: Georgetown Book Warehouse, 34 Armstrong Avenue, Georgetown, Ontario L7G 4R9. Call toll-free: 1-800-247-7160.

Books can be purchased at your bookstore or directly from Barron's. Enclose check or money order for total amount plus sales tax where applicable and 10% for postage (minimum charge $3.75. Can. $4.00). All major credit cards are accepted. Prices subject to change without notice. ISBN Prefix: 0-8120   (#64) R7/95